The Bennett Law Controversy in Wisconsin

May 24, 2011

Dear Rosalie and Dick,

Thank you for your interest in my book. You and your family are so special to me! Thank you also for welcoming me into your lives. I am truly blessed by your friendship.

Love,
Janet

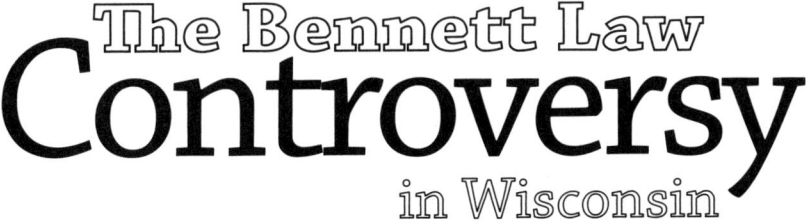

The Bennett Law Controversy in Wisconsin

A Study of
AMERICANIZATION
among **IMMIGRANT** *Populations*

By Janet Wegner Johnston

SIGNAL PEAK PRESS
Casa Grande, Arizona

Copyright 2011 by Janet Wegner Johnston. All rights reserved, including the right to reproduce this book, photographs, or portions thereof in any form without written permission from the publisher.

Published by Signal Peak Press LLC
P.O. Box 11107
Casa Grande, Arizona 85130
520-709-6658

Cover Art, Cover Illustration(s), and Cover Design Copyright 2011 by Signal Peak Press LLC
Cover Design, Book Design, Typesetting, and Computer Graphics by Jayme Fraser

Library of Congress Control Number: 2011926568

ISBN: 978-1-879915-25-1

Manufactured in the United States of America

To the Memory of My Father and Mother
Herbert and Adeline Wegner

Table of Contents

List of Tables viii
Foreword ix
Preface xiii
Acknowledgments xvii
Introduction xix
CHAPTERS
    I. The Origin of the Wisconsin Bennett Law 1
    II. Sources of Opposition 11
    III. Background of the "Americanization" Issue 19
    IV. The Anti-Bennett Law Campaign Begins 37
    V. The Bennett Law Controversy in Politics 57
    VI. Reactions of Other Religious Denominations and
        Nationality Groups 87
    VII. The Defeat of the Bennett Law 99
    VIII. Bennett Law Debate as it Relates to U.S. Church-State
        Relations 127
Appendix I 137
Appendix II 143
Bibliographical Note 147
Bibliography 163
About the Author 183

List of Tables

1. The Native Origin and Population of Foreign-Born Residents of Wisconsin in 1890 173

2. Percentage of German-Born in Wisconsin's Total Population and in the Total Foreign-Born Population of the State, 1850-1890 174

3. Comparative School Census Statistics for Children of Wisconsin between the Ages of 7 and 14, 1889-1890 175

4. Ratio of Democratic Vote in 1890 to Democratic Vote in 1888. Same as to Republican Vote 176

5. Election Pluralities by County and Party in the Wisconsin Gubernatorial Contest for the Years 1886-1894 179

Foreword

The United States has long prided itself on the fact that it has been a "melting pot" for many immigrant groups. Europeans from many countries—Germany, France, England, Italy, to name just a few—came to this land throughout the nineteenth century and contributed their share to the dominant culture. Scandinavian countries such as Norway, Sweden, and Finland also provided settlers to the Midwestern states where northern European immigrants predominated. Asian immigrants from China and Japan—although smaller in numbers and concentrated in Western states such as California—also added to the total population. Much earlier, Spanish Conquistadors conquered the native peoples of the Southwest and imprinted their culture on the western part of the United States and Mexico.

Over time, these disparate peoples—speaking different languages, attending a variety of churches, both Protestant and Catholic, and insofar as possible holding tightly to their own customs and traditions—were able to create the culture that Americans currently celebrate. It was, however, not an easy transition for many of these early settlers. Clashes of culture arose between the first immigrants, largely of English descent, and those who came later, most often from northern European countries.

The following discussion of the Bennett Law controversy in Wisconsin, which began with the law's enactment in 1889, spells out in considerable detail one such clash between a large contingent of German immigrants and their fellow English-speaking citizens. Originally intended as a straightforward compulsory education act to keep young immigrants in school and out of factories, the seemingly innocuous addition of the words "in the English language" to the teaching requirement ignited a firestorm of protest, primarily among German-Americans, many of whom attended private, parochial schools established by the Catholic Church. It was believed by many of these recent immigrants that the intent of the law was to undermine their schools and churches, and they fought back vociferously.

During the controversy, Governor William D. Hoard, a Republican, who strongly supported the law, was vilified, while Democrats, who generally opposed the bill, and the Republicans, who had supported it, fought bitterly. Those in favor of the law were seen as anti-immigrant by many Germans, and so they worked diligently and in the end successfully, to defeat the governor in the next election (1890) and to repeal the law.

The following pages outline the controversy and its results in the State of Wisconsin between the time the law was enacted in 1889 and repealed in 1891. The analysis of this controversy was prepared as part of the requirements for a master's degree in history at Brown University in 1966. Despite the passage of years since then, I believe that the facts of this case have relevance to the situation today when another issue involving immigrants—in this case, a large number of Spanish-speaking immigrants (some legal, some not) have been crossing the border from Mexico into Arizona, New Mexico, and Texas.

The issues involved in this later influx of immigrants to the United States are reminiscent of those arising in Wisconsin during the 1890s and are even more complex. Nonetheless, I believe that this is not the time to give in to simplistic solutions or harsh judgments about the people involved in the crisis. The situation needs to be resolved in a clear-headed manner without resorting to nativist threats and punitive solutions. As the history of Wisconsin's Bennett Law and its ultimate repeal clearly illustrates, a more measured approach to immigration conflicts is better suited to the ultimate well-being of all the citizens of this great country.

Preface

The Bennett Law Controversy in Wisconsin is an analysis of a pivotal moment in the state's history when concern for Americanization of recent European immigrants clashed with an equally valid interest in ensuring a proper balance between church and state responsibilities and authority. The contest between these two opposing objectives led to two years of political unrest, which ultimately resulted in the defeat of the governor who had insisted on the need to require a working knowledge of English among Wisconsin's immigrant population.

Although Wisconsin's political turmoil began in 1889 and ended in 1891 with the repeal of the Bennett Law, the issues that were the center of attention in these early years have not entirely disappeared from our national discourse. Nowhere is this more apparent than the current controversy swirling around the enactment of Senate Bill (S.B.) 1070 (officially entitled "The Support Our Law Enforcement and Safe Neighborhoods Act") in Arizona this past year. Although opposed by the Arizona

Catholic Conference and other interested parties, the Act was signed into law by Governor Jan Brewer on April 23, 2010.

The new law has been described as "the broadest and strictest anti-illegal immigration measure in decades" and has prompted other states to consider adopting similar legislation. Current federal legislation requires certain aliens to register with the U.S. government and to keep registration documents in their possession at all times. The new Arizona law enhances this requirement by making it a state misdemeanor crime for any alien to be in Arizona without such documentation. It also bars state or local officials and agencies from restricting the enforcement of federal immigration laws, directs employers to keep verification records of their employees' work eligibility, and makes it a felony for employers not to verify their employees' eligibility to work in this country. Finally, the legislation allows law enforcement officers, without a warrant, to arrest any person if the officer has probable cause to believe that the person has committed any public offense that makes the person removable from the United States.

All of this is taking place at a time when there are deep concerns within the state about the effect of allowing immigrants, particularly those from Mexico and other Latin American nations, to perpetuate their language and customs in the United States. This concern is one that clearly parallels the situation in Wisconsin in 1889, when Governor William Dempster Hoard and others sought to address their concerns about the need for immigrants to become "Americanized" by the enactment of the Bennett Law, which required that instruction in all schools, including those administered by church officials, be given in the English language.

It is hoped that publishing this research about my home state will help to remind all parties involved in the current Arizona crisis that moderation in speech and action is crucial to an outcome that is acceptable to all parties engaged in the debate. If the information presented in this book can encourage these parties to modify their stridency and search for common ground that will end the controversy, it will have served a useful purpose.

Acknowledgments

I would like to thank Professor Jay Fraser and my fellow students in his publishing class at Central Arizona College for their encouragement in finishing this book, which was originally written to fulfill the requirements for a master's degree in American history at Brown University in 1966. I had taken Professor Fraser's class in hopes of assisting a friend's son who was in the process of writing a novel, but when I discovered that the timetable for that publication was going to be delayed, I needed an immediate replacement assignment for the writing workshop. After some careful consideration, I decided to focus on my earlier analysis of the controversy surrounding the Bennett Law—a compulsory education act passed in Wisconsin in 1889 that required instruction in the English language. The result of that effort is this book.

Although my wonderful parents, Herbert and Adeline Wegner, have already passed away, I would be remiss if I did not acknowledge their continuing love and encouragement throughout my own life. They supported my desire for a college education in every way that they could and made sure that I had ample time for studying and otherwise working toward my dreams. Because of their efforts on my behalf, I went on to earn an undergraduate degree in history and English from the University of Wisconsin, a master's degree in history from Brown, and eventually a Ph.D. in political science and public policy from the University of Chicago.

At all these institutions, I had the benefit of enthusiastic professors (including Dr. William G. McLoughlin, my thesis adviser at Brown) who worked hard to instill in me their own extensive knowledge of history and government, which later led to a satisfying career at the U.S. Department of Labor and the National Commission for Employment Policy in Washington, D.C.

To all the supportive people who throughout my life have encouraged me to achieve my goals for the future and have assisted me in that endeavor, I acknowledge your efforts on my behalf and offer my sincere thanks.

Introduction

In the history of church-state relations in the United States, one of the most frequent realms of controversy has been the field of education. Religious groups, anxious to instill in their young people high moral standards and an understanding of their own church creeds, have long relied on their parochial schools to ensure such training, along with regular secular instruction. On the other hand, since the development of the public school system in the 1840s, the state has also sought to supply its own need for a well-educated and responsible citizenry through the passage of compulsory education acts.

These laws, varying from state to state, have occasionally been so severe that, as in the case of an Oregon statute later declared unconstitutional, *all* children were compelled to attend public schools. Other states at various times have required that as many weeks be taught in private schools as in public, that all teachers be certified, that particular courses such as American history and civics be included in the curriculum, that public and parochial schools be equivalent, etc. In some cases the state has also required the inspection of private institutions to certify compliance with these rules. Such measures, however, have had within them the seeds of controversy, for religious groups—long accustomed to governing their own denominational schools under rights guaranteed by the First Amendment to the Constitution—have often shown themselves to be reluctant to accept such regulation from the outside.

One of the earliest of these compulsory education laws and surely one of the most controversial was "An Act concerning the education and employment of children" (the so-called Bennett Law) passed in Wisconsin in 1889. Although ostensibly a simple measure to guarantee a minimum of instruction for all children between the ages of seven and fourteen and, at the same time, check the spread of child labor, it aroused such intense opposition from among certain religious groups and nationalities in the state that the Republican governor who had supported it was completely overwhelmed by his opponent in the next election and the law itself was repealed in 1891.

The source of this great antagonism was undoubtedly the provision of the act that required that certain subjects be taught "in the English language" for at least twelve weeks of the year. Among the large foreign-born population of Wisconsin, particularly the Germans, this clause represented a clear threat of encroachment by the state upon their right to educate their children in schools of their own choosing. Indeed, it was feared by many of the law's opponents that it was deliberately aimed at destroying Catholic and Lutheran parochial schools, many of which taught in German or some other European tongue. In the bitter political campaign that followed the passage of the law, therefore, resistance to "State paternalism" became a rallying cry for those who opposed it.

Nevertheless, an examination of the Bennett Law controversy raises serious questions about the validity of any unqualified assertion that this was simply a case of unwarranted state interference with religious institutions, as some historians have previously suggested. Why, for example, had the main opposition derived from the German population (both Protestant and Catholic), while many Irish Catholics, Scandinavian Lutherans, and English-speaking Protestants actively supported the measure? How does this controversy in Wisconsin relate to similar controversies elsewhere in the United States at this time such as "Cahenslyism," "Americanism," the A.P.A. movement, Prohibition, and child labor? What precisely were the arguments presented by opponents of the law, and how did its originators defend their actions?

It is with these questions that the following discussion of the Bennett Law will deal, and it is hoped that in the end the actual complex nature of the problem will have become apparent, along with a greater understanding of its significance in the history of church-state relations within the United States. Although the arguments against the law presented during the controversy spoke harshly of state paternalism and interference with the right of religious conscience, the conclusion reached here is that the incident was less a matter of religion or of education than of German resistance to assimilation.

The problems of acculturation that beset many immigrant churches in this period, resulting in various forms of dissension within the denominations themselves, such as the Cahensly movement within the Catholic Church, were manifested politically in a determination of many immigrants to oppose any law that would, as they put it, forcibly "denationalize" them. Above all, they were resolved to preserve for their children, the culture, language, and traditions of the fatherland. As a potential threat to this heritage, therefore, the Bennett Law could not be tolerated.

The Bennett Law Controversy
in Wisconsin

The Origin of the Wisconsin Bennett Law

As early as 1879, Wisconsin had seen the need for a compulsory education measure when a statute was enacted requiring the attendance of all children (excepting those with excuses permissible to the school board) between the ages of seven and fifteen years at some public or private school.[1] That this law was not properly enforced, however, became readily apparent when Jesse B. Thayer, State Superintendent of Public Instruction, issued his biennial report for 1887-88. Statistics revealed that from 40,000 to 50,000 children between the ages of seven and fourteen attended no school whatsoever, while the total number of children in the state who attended some school was actually decreasing in comparison with an overall yearly increase of population in that age group.[2]

---

1   Wisconsin, *The Laws of Wisconsin*, I (Madison, 1879), 155-156.
2   Wisconsin, Department of Public Instruction, "Biennial Report of the State Superintendent of Wisconsin for the Years 1887-1888" in *Wisconsin Governor's Message and Accompanying Documents (1887-1888)*, I (Madison, 1889), 17-20. It was later claimed by opponents of the Bennett Law that these figures failed to take into account the full number of children attending private and parochial schools, so the figure of 50,000 was grossly exaggerated. See, for example,

At the same time, reports revealed that some Americans born in this country of immigrant parents could not read, write, or even speak the English language.[3] Interpreters were needed and appointed as regular court officers, paid from public funds, in the courts of certain counties so that native-born Americans could give testimony. At times, even juries consisted of non-English speaking Americans. Moreover, a number of Wisconsin towns kept their records entirely in German, and many of the parochial schools maintained by the Catholic and Lutheran churches (at least 129 according to statistics provided by the *Germania*, a leading German language paper in the state) taught no English at all. In fact, in several county districts where the German element predominated, even public school instruction was being provided in German.[4]

Christian Koerner, *The Bennett Law and the German Parochial Schools of Wisconsin* (Milwaukee, 1890) [pamphlet in the possession of the Wisconsin Historical Society of Madison] and the *Madison Daily Democrat*, April 11, 1890, p. 1. Nevertheless, estimation procedures of private school enrollment by the opposition were equally arbitrary and subject to error, and in any case it was clear to the act's supporters that a large number of children who by the law of 1879 should have been in school were not. Many of these, they feared, were swelling the child labor force in factories.

3 At least one opponent of the law argued from the standpoint that since in many communities German was the only language in use, there was no need for children to learn English. Letter published in the *Milwaukee Sentinel*, February 12, 1890, p. 4.

4 During the Bennett Law controversy a number of cases involving the need for court interpreters came to light. One court officer of the Fifteenth Judicial Circuit reported in a letter to the *Milwaukee Sentinel*, March 22, 1890, p.4, several examples known to him personally that had occurred throughout Wisconsin. The town of Stettin in Marathon County was the one most often referred to as a case where official records were kept entirely in German, and numerous examples were found to substantiate the charge that many parochial schools did not include the English language in their curriculum. Michael Bennett, himself, spoke of two such schools in his own district. See the *Private Letter Books of William D. Hoard* (MSS. in possession of the Wisconsin Historical Society) 16 (1890, Jan. 29 – 1890, May 12), 314-315; 18 (1890, Sept. 13 – 1891, Dec.

Governor William Dempster Hoard relied heavily on these facts and statistics when he recommended in his annual opening address to the Legislature in 1889 that a new law be enacted to halt the spread of illiteracy, prevent children from swelling the ranks of factory labor, and provide all young people with the fundamental language tools necessary for successful competition in the adult world. Speaking before the assembled body on January 10, 1889, he said:

> The child that is, the citizen that is to be, has a right to demand of the State that it be provided, as against all contingencies, with a reasonable amount of instruction in common English branches. Especially has it the right to demand that it be provided with the ability to read and write the language of this country. In this connection, I would recommend such legislation as would make it the duty of county and city superintendents to inspect all schools for the purpose and with the authority to require that reading and writing in English be daily taught therein.[5]

With these words, Governor Hoard set in motion the legislation that was to culminate in a statewide controversy of significance to the history of church-state relationships in the United States and that was to be largely responsible for his own defeat as governor of Wisconsin in 1890.

The first ill-fated legislation providing for the suggested inspection was introduced into the Senate on February 13, 1889, in the form of a bill written by Senator Levi E. Pond of Westfield, Wisconsin. His bill called for annual reports from private and denominational schools on blanks provided by the office of the State Superintendent

---

20), 114-115, 140-141. George W. Rankin, *William Dempster Hoard* (Fort Atkinson, Wis., 1925), p. 129. Reprint of the *Janesville Gazette* in the *Milwaukee Sentinel*, October 11, 1889, p. 2.

5 Wisconsin, *Wisconsin Governor's Message and Accompanying Documents*, I (Madison, 1889), 17.

of Public Instruction, listing the number of students between the ages of four and twenty who were in attendance during the year, the subjects taught with the number enrolled in each, and whether or not instruction was being provided in the English language. This information was to be included in the biennial report of the superintendent, and any individual refusing to comply would be subject to a $10 fine for each offense.[6]

Response to the proposed legislation was swift and complete. Almost immediately over 40,000 signatures on petitions from every corner of the state, from clergymen and laymen alike, began pouring into the Assembly and Senate. Delegations opposing the bill journeyed to the capitol at Madison to protest what they believed to be an unwarranted assumption of control by the state over their own private denominational schools.[7] Fraught with significance for events to come, these protests declared:

> There is at present no good reason for the proposed measure. The bill will cause in the end a conflict between state and church, which all good citizens and friends of personal liberty would sincerely deprecate. The bill tends in the direction of state supervision over parochial schools and may lead to vexatious relations between church and state in the matter of education. The bill evidently implies more than it says—it seems to be intended as a feeler or entering wedge for more effective measures.[8]

Faced with this overwhelming opposition, the Committee on Education reported the bill back for indefinite postponement

---

6 Wisconsin, *Senate Journal* (Madison, 1889), pp. 162, 824-825.
7 August C. Stellhorn, *Schools of the Lutheran Church—Missouri Synod* (St. Louis, 1963), p. 236. See list of petitions in Wisconsin *Assembly Journal* (Madison, 1889), pp. 308-314 (Index) and *Senate Journal*, 1889, pp. 180-191 (Index).
8 *Milwaukee Journal*, October 22, 1890, p. 4.

on March 13, as did the Judiciary Committee three weeks later. Senator Pond, however, managed to have the bill laid over until April 12, when he could propose amendments. Then, on the following day, with himself as a committee of one, he presented a long and extensive defense of the proposed measure, chiefly on the grounds that on the part of church leaders there was a complete "misapprehension of the purposes and aims of the bill." Nevertheless, in the end, he was forced to pocket the measure, and no further mention of it is evidenced after April 13.[9]

In view of the overwhelmingly negative reaction to the Pond bill, it seems incredible that the Bennett Law introduced in the Assembly at almost the same time, on February 20, 1889, should have elicited no public response at all, particularly when it is understood that a committee of Lutherans had anxiously inquired among several members of the Legislature whether any bills kindred to the Pond measure had been proposed.[10]

In truth, unlike the earlier bill, the Bennett proposal did not demand inspection of private and parochial schools. Rather, it required simply that every child between the ages of seven and fourteen attend some school "public or private" for not less than twelve weeks of each year, with parents or guardians subject to fines of up to $20 for each refusal to comply. Local school district boards were entrusted with the responsibility of enforcing this provision, and only they could initiate complaints for noncompliance.

Later sections of the bill provided against truancy and the employment of children below the age of thirteen in factories,

---

9 *Senate Journal*, 1889, pp. 162 (introduction of bill to the Senate), 636, 639, 722, 750, 824-826 (amended bill proposed), 828-833 (committee of one report).
10 *Milwaukee Journal*, March 25, 1890, p. 4.

mines, or other businesses. More importantly, Section 5, which was to prove the chief bone of contention to German religious groups, declared that "no school shall be regarded as a school, under this act, unless there shall be taught therein, as part of the elementary education of children, reading, writing, arithmetic, and United States history, *in the English language*" (italics added).[11] (See Appendix for full text.)

At the time, however, any potentially objectionable features of the bill apparently escaped notice. The record of its passage in the journal of both houses of the Legislature reads like a textbook summary of lawmaking procedure. It is interesting, for example, that on March 26, three days before the Pond bill was reported on adversely by the Senate Committee on Education, the Bennett proposal was reported out favorably by its counterpart in the Assembly. On April 6, the same day the Senate measure was laid over for a week, the Bennett bill was passed by the lower house. In all this time, moreover, there was no recorded debate about the bill in either chamber.

The only petition on record pertaining to the measure was one signed by a thousand Milwaukee citizens who *favored* the passage of the compulsory education bill.[12] In the end, the law was passed without a single dissenting vote and routinely signed by the Governor on April 18, 1889. On record in support of the measure were 95 Republicans, 35 Democrats, one Independent, and two Laborites, among whom were many representatives of the two groups that ultimately led the opposition to the law—viz., German Catholics and German Lutherans.[13] Even the Wisconsin Teachers'

---

11 Wisconsin, *The Laws of Wisconsin*, I (Madison, 1889), 729-733 (Chapter 519).
12 *Assembly Journal*, 1889, p. 517.
13 *Senate Journal*, 1889, p. 878 and *Assembly Journal*, 1889, pp. 1017, 1224.

Association accepted the law as a benefit to the community and endorsed the measure unanimously.[14]

It was later charged that the law had been "slyly engineered through," that the Pond bill had been a decoy, an intentional smoke screen device aimed at securing the easy passage of an even more objectionable law. Yet there is no evidence to substantiate this belief. Rather, as Michael J. Bennett, the Assemblyman who introduced the bill, himself clearly stated, "every member of the legislature was given ample opportunity to read it and determine its scope and object for himself." He personally had sent out 300 copies of the bill to prominent educators throughout the state, requesting their opinion of the measure. In each case of a reply, the opinion rendered was favorable to the proposed law. Even the *Germania*, whose legal editor Christian Koerner eventually headed the anti-Bennett Law forces in the state, had received a copy, but no comment either for or against the bill was forthcoming. Clearly, no matter how objectionable the statute later appeared to some, initially no voice was heard to oppose it.[15]

Nor, indeed, is there any concrete evidence to substantiate the allegation—made at the time and repeated by a Lutheran church historian as late as 1963—that the true author of the bill had been the Committee of One Hundred, a Boston Know-Nothing group.[16] In actual fact, the need for such a measure had been

---

Senator William Kennedy, a Democrat and a member of the committee on education for the upper house, later claimed he had voted against the bill. The *Senate Journal* (p. 853) does record his dissent from the favorable reportage of the bill out of the education committee, but there are no votes recorded against the bill in its final passage in the upper house.

14 *Milwaukee Sentinel*, December 29, 1889, p. 6.
15 Letter from Michael J. Bennett, October 26, 1889, published in the *Milwaukee Sentinel*, October 28, 1889, p. 2. See also *Milwaukee Sentinel*, March 11, 1890, p. 4.
16 Stellhorn, p. 237. See also, e.g., *Der Herold*, October 10, 1889, translated

suggested by members of the North Side Turners' Association of Milwaukee, an organization composed of liberal-minded Germans who believed that advancement in the new land demanded a sound education and knowledge of the English language. An interview published in the *Milwaukee Sentinel* in March 1980, establishes the fact that several of these Turners who were also members of the Tenth District School Association of Milwaukee had initiated the idea for such a law, when it became apparent that in their district alone child labor was keeping from 3,400 to 3,500 children out of a total of 7,000 from attending any school whatsoever. Frank Sebastian, President of the School Society, made their motives clear when he stated emphatically: "The purpose of the bill . . . was to knock child labor in the head and to make it compulsory for all children under 14 years of age to attend school. To keep them out of factories was the main object of the bill."[17]

It was toward this end, that members of the Turners' Association, having been informed by one legislator that the 1879 compulsory education act had become a dead letter, approached Robert Luscombe, Assistant City Attorney for Milwaukee, to draw up a more effectual statute for submission to the Wisconsin legislature. This he did, devoting several weeks to the project, although Governor Hoard later admitted to having written the troublesome English-language clause (Section 5) himself. It is interesting to note also that the bill was read by most of the people in the district and approved despite the fact that the majority were German Lutherans.[18]

---

by the *Milwaukee Sentinel*, October 11, 1889, p. 2.
17 *Milwaukee Sentinel*, March 13, 1890, p. 1.
18 *Milwaukee Sentinel*, March 11, 1890, p. 4. The governor's admission that he wrote the controversial English language clause himself can be found in Louise Phelps Kellogg, "Notes of an Interview with Ex-Governor William Dempster

Finally, the bill was ready for submission, but as Luscombe later explained, although the measure was primarily designed for Milwaukee, it was hoped that prejudice against the labor element could be avoided by having it introduced by a rural member of the legislature. It was ultimately for this reason that Michael John Bennett, a representative from Pine Knot, Iowa County, a former school teacher, an Irish Catholic, and the chairman of the Assembly's Committee on Education, agreed to sponsor the bill, while in the Senate, the chairman of a parallel committee, Christian Wydule, a German Lutheran from Milwaukee, introduced and supported the measure.[19]

In drawing up the bill, Luscombe followed closely similar enactments in Illinois and Ohio, which in turn were modeled after statutes recorded in New York and Massachusetts.[20] Opposition to the Edwards Act in the neighboring state of Illinois, which also passed unanimously in 1889, helped defeat one year later the Republican Party, which had sponsored it and subsequently resulted in the law's repeal in 1893.[21]

This outcome not only mirrors the eventual resolution of the Bennett Law controversy, but at the same time illustrates the fact that the problems involving "Americanization" of immigrants

Hoard," at his home at Fort Atkinson, August 12 and August 13, 1918 [MS in possession of Wisconsin State Historical Society], p. 2, in Kellogg Papers.
19 *Milwaukee Sentinel*, March 11, 1890, p.4.
20 It is possible that the similarities between the Massachusetts and Wisconsin enactments gave some apparent credibility to the otherwise unwarranted assumption that a Boston Know-Nothing group had been the "true" author of the Wisconsin statute.
21 Because of the close parallel between the two measures and their consequences, Wisconsin newspapers gave considerable coverage to the situation in the neighboring state. A copy of the Edwards Bill can be found in the *Madison Daily Democrat*, May 10, 1890, p. 7, and other articles concerning the measure are available in the *Wisconsin State Journal, Milwaukee Sentinel*, and *Milwaukee Journal* for the year 1890. See also Stellhorn, pp. 244-245.

were not confined to the particular state of Wisconsin. Rather, wherever were found large settlements of newly arrived foreign-born citizens, particularly those who by language differences were cut off from the rest of the English-speaking population, there a potential source of unrest and controversy existed. Although their children might seek to accommodate themselves to the new land as rapidly as possible, the first generation immigrant would resist, maintaining stubbornly the religious customs and traditions as well as the language of his fatherland. Any state law that seemingly infringed on these areas was, consequently, subject to suspicion and attack.[22]

---

22 Interesting discussions of the problem faced by immigrant churches of accommodating themselves to conditions in America can be found in Will Herberg, *Protestant-Catholic-Jew* (New York, Doubleday Anchor Paperback, 1960) and H. Richard Niebuhr, *The Social Sources of Denominationalism* (Cleveland and New York, Meridian Paperback, 1964), pp. 200-235.

II
Sources of Opposition

With this fact in mind, it is not then surprising to find that major opposition to the law stemmed initially from three sources: German Catholics, German Lutherans, and their chief organs, the German-language journals and newspapers.[23] Among the latter, the *Germania*, a Lutheran weekly owned by George Brumder and edited by George Koeppen led the fight, with its legal editor Christian Koerner, the commander of all anti-Bennett Law forces.

Also joining in the debate were two weeklies—the *Excelsior* and the *Columbia*, both Catholic journals, and two secular daily papers—the *Herold*, Republican in its leanings, and the *Seebote*, an independent Democratic organ. It was these papers, particularly the *Germania*, which carried the fight to their readers and

---

23 This book focuses its attention primarily on the German Catholics and German Lutherans, who initiated and led the opposition against the Bennett Law. Nevertheless, both the German Evangelical Church and the German Reformed Church were in agreement with their stand. See *Milwaukee Journal*, June 5, 1890, p. 4. The Germans of whatever religion formed almost a solid bloc in opposition to what they believed to be a threat to their language and traditions.

ultimately rallied them into an almost solid bloc of votes opposed to the compulsory education measure.

In the ensuing controversy, several specific provisions within the law were singled out as particularly harmful to the two religious groups involved. First among these was the district clause in Section 1 of the act, which stated that each child affected by the law must attend a private or public school "in the city, town, or district in which he resides." This provision was taken as a deliberate "stab" at the parochial schools, because it was pointed out by the law's opponents that public and parochial school districts were not identical in their boundaries. Thus, it often happened that a parochial school was not located in the district where a child resided, and one school would enroll children from several public school districts. If the law were followed to the letter, new schools would have to be built in the various districts where none existed previously, old schools would lose many former students, and three or four teachers would be needed where one had served before. This argument was particularly effective among the Scandinavian Lutherans who were able to afford only a few schools of their own, but who otherwise were less concerned about the language provision than their German brethren and consequently less inclined to see the danger of the new compulsory education law.[24]

The distress excited by this provision is particularly apparent in a pamphlet entitled *The Bennett Law and the German Parochial Schools of Wisconsin*, written by Christian Koerner and published by the *Germania*. Koerner declared that because of Section 5 parents henceforth would be unable to send their children to a city school if they lived in the country, to Lutheran colleges at

---

24 Rasmus B. Anderson, *The Life Story of Rasmus B. Anderson as told by himself with the assistance of Albert O. Barton* (Madison, 1917), pp. 594-600, esp. pp. 595-596.

Watertown and Milwaukee, or even back to Germany for the benefit of an Old-World education. "What a herd of white slaves this law makes of us!" he cried.[25]

In vain did Governor Hoard and other supporters of the law point out that this was not the intention of the act, that in any case this provision was not essential to the measure, and that they would accept any reasonable amendments that still maintained the basic principle of the statute—viz., "the *duty* of the State to require, and the *right* of the children of the State to receive, instruction in the language of the country."[26] Far from wishing to undermine denominational schools, Governor Hoard insisted it did not matter in the least whether such knowledge was acquired "in the private school, the public school, or at the child's home." The question at issue was not where such instruction could be achieved, but only that all children should receive at least some.[27]

In addition to the district clause, however, opponents insisted that fines for disobedience to the law, which reached a maximum of $20 for *each* offense, were extreme and under its provisions school boards were given far too much power. It was feared that members of district school boards, hostile to the Germans and to their religion, would seek to "strangle and annihilate" their parochial schools by denying that such were really schools under the law, and actual cases of such unfair rulings were alleged to have occurred in Illinois. Moreover, it was believed that parents would lose their right to trial

---

25 Koerner, *The Bennett Law*, p. 19.
26 Interview with Governor William D. Hoard in the *Milwaukee Journal*, May 5, 1980, p. 1. Letter to Andrew D. Agnew, President of the Young Men's Republican Club of Milwaukee, dated October 7, 1890, in Hoard, *Private Letter Books*, 18:173-174.
27 Letter to R.J. Matthias of Manawa, WI, in Hoard, *Private Letter Books*, 17 (1890, May 31 – 1890, Sept. 13), 287-288.

by jury because they must present their reasons for keeping a child out of school not to a court but rather to the district school board.[28]

All of these fears and objections, however, were united under one rallying cry—Resist the paternalism of the state! A deep feeling was spreading among the Catholics and Lutherans of Wisconsin that the state was unjustly trying to meddle in church affairs and was interfering with parental authority over their own children. Members of both these religions protested that since they paid taxes for public schools as well as for their own private denominational schools, the state had no right to intervene with regard to curriculum or any other policy.

Typical of their reaction was the declaration unanimously adopted by the Evangelical Lutheran Synod of Wisconsin and other states, meeting at Milwaukee in June, 1889:

> We are not enemies of the public schools; we consider them and declare them to be a necessary institution. We are ever willing to pay our taxes for the support of the public schools. We are opposed to any and every grant of public school funds to private schools.—But we insist upon enjoying the privileges of founding private schools with our own means; of regulating and governing them, without external interference, according to our convictions and according to sound principles of pedagogy, for the sake of making our children loyal and good citizens.[29]

Among other opponents of the law, both religious and secular, it appears that this question of state paternalism was the decisive issue in eliciting their opposition to the measure. Educators such as President Edward H. Merrell of Ripon College, Professor A. F.

---

28 Koerner, *The Bennett Law*, pp. 14-19. *The Underlying Principles of the Bennett Law* (n.p.,n.d.), pp. 2-3 [an anti-Bennett campaign pamphlet preserved in the Wisconsin Historical Society].
29 Quoted in Koerner, *The Bennett Law*, p. 12.

North of Northwestern College at Waukesha, and even John Fiske of Harvard agreed that the government had overstepped its proper sphere of action, and, thus, in the words of Professor North, it was time to "set our faces as a flint against the tyranny of paternalism and in defense of the rights of the individual."

A similar concern undoubtedly motivated Wisconsin's Seventh Day Adventist Tract and Missionary Society to go on record against all religious legislation by a civil government and resulted in editorial comment by the *New York Evangelist*, a Presbyterian organ, and the *Western Recorder*, of Louisville, Kentucky, published under the auspices of the Baptist Church. These three churches had a long history of opposition to state control, and it is not surprising that any law which they believed to be a potential threat to their religious liberty was subject to immediate attack.[30]

However, despite the constant denials of German religious groups and the fact that almost all formal protests were made on the basis of resistance to state paternalism alone, it was clear that a very deep and central concern of the law's opponents involved the English language section of the Act. In fact, wrote the Manitowoc County *Chronicle*, "Strike the two words 'in English' from the law and not a churchman in the State could be found to raise his voice against it."[31]

---

30 *Milwaukee Journal*, May 2, 1980, p. 4; May 10, p. 1; May 27, p. 2; August 20, p. 3; October 11, p. 1. *Madison Daily Democrat*, October 9, 1989, p. 1; May 2, 1890, p. 4; June 13, p. 1. *A Presbyterian on the Bennett Law* (n.p., n.d.) and *A Baptist Opinion on the Bennett Law* (n.p., n.d.) [two campaign pamphlets now in the possession of the Wisconsin Historical Society].

31 Reprinted in the *Milwaukee Sentinel*, October 4, 1889, p. 4. Edward Gillen, a prominent Roman Catholic from Racine, Wisconsin, used almost these exact words in a speech at Father Matthew Hall in Racine in October, 1890. At that time, he stated that the new law had been discussed by different Catholic clergymen and laymen in his city, including the president of one Catholic college, and had been generally accepted as a good law. In fact, Gillen declared, "'I am fully satisfied in my own mind that if the word English, or the teaching of

Charges of "nativism" and "Know-Nothingism" rose to meet all those who sought to ensure a universal knowledge of English, while the words, "*Unser sprache und sitten, die geben wir nicht hin,*" ("We will not surrender our language and customs.") became a byword among German voters.[32] Indeed, it appeared self-evident to men like Christian Koerner that "having been spoken for centuries by a not inconsiderable number of the population of the Old Colonies and of the revolutionary heroes, and at present by millions of the inhabitants of the States and Territories—it is no more a *foreign* language than the English language, which like the German was not spoken by the natives of this Country, but was imported from foreign lands."[33]

For their part, however, defenders of the Bennett Law insisted that a knowledge of English was essential for successful competition in American society, as well as for the practice of intelligent citizenship. "The friends of compulsory education have no desire to interfere with the private or parochial schools in any manner whatsoever," said Governor Hoard. "They only ask that all children shall have an equal opportunity for advancement, and they cannot have such an opportunity without a knowledge of the language in the country."[34]

The German religious leaders and newspaper editors who opposed the law—it was believed by the Governor and his supporters—were motivated less by a concern for the rights of parents or the welfare of their children than by a selfish desire to maintain their control in the churches or a large circulation for

---

English, was stricken out of the Bennett law, we would not have heard anything from the German Catholic bishops or priests.'" He believed the same to be true of the Lutheran clergymen. See *Milwaukee Sentinel*, November 1, 1890, p. 1.
32 *Germania*, March 28, 1890; also quoted in Rankin, p. 129.
33 Koerner, *The Bennett Law*, p. 10.
34 Hoard, *Private Letter Books*, 17:287-288.

their newspapers. To supporters of the law, their position seemed a clear case of self-interest arising from a stubborn resistance to Americanization.

Thus, not only was it believed at the time by proponents of the law, but it would seem clear to the modern student of American religious history familiar with the problems faced by the immigrant churches in this period, that such opposition to Americanization was as important to the Bennett Law controversy as the issue of determining proper bounds in church-state relationships. Moreover, the reason for this becomes readily apparent when one examines the history of Wisconsin's foreign population and, in particular, those of German origin.

III
Background of the "Americanization" Issue

In 1890, 63 percent of Wisconsin's population was composed of persons of foreign birth or their children. The census of that year reported a total of 519,199 foreign-born residents, including 282,900 from Germanic nations (among which Germany itself ranked first with 259,819); 99,838 from Scandinavian nations; 99,888 from the British dominions; 32,424 from Slavic nations; and 3,189 from Latin nations. See Table 1.

The number of German immigrants alone equaled half (50.04%) the total of all other foreign-born citizens and represented 15.4 percent of Wisconsin's total population of 1,686,880. Moreover, when the number of native-born with both parents German is added to the number of actual German-born citizens, the result is even higher—551,834 persons, or 32.7 percent of the state's entire population. Wisconsin thus had a larger percentage of German-born residents than any other state and stood third, surpassed only by New York and Illinois, in its total of German-born population.[35] See Table 2.

---

35 U.S. Bureau of the Census, *Eleventh Census of the U.S.—1890: Part I,*

With regard to religious affiliation, there were in Wisconsin approximately 325,000 Roman Catholics of whom about 114,000 were German-speaking. In the various Lutheran and Evangelical synods represented in the state, some 148,911 members were listed in the Census of 1890, with approximately 95,000 of these included in bodies where German was the main language in use. Among these two religious groups, about 50,000 to 60,000 Catholics and 40,000 Lutherans were of voting age. Clearly, in Wisconsin where the total Presidential vote of 1888 was 354,515, the Germans of whatever faith were a political force to be reckoned with, and any issue that could unite their votes into a solid bloc for or against a particular party or measure was a matter of grave concern to political leaders.[36]

Population (Washington, D.C., 1895), pp. cxlvi, 606-609, 682-697. The actual number of native whites with both parents born in some foreign country in Wisconsin in 1890 was 1,067,186. An additional 43,233 (not included in the above designated 63%) had at least one parent of foreign birth. The other figures presented refer to Germany alone. The total number of German-speaking immigrants (i.e., all those grouped under the general heading of Germanic nations) represented 16.78% of the state's total population and 54.51% of all other foreign-born citizens.

36 U.S. Bureau of the Census, *Census Bulletins: "Statistics of Churches"* (Washington, D.C., 1891), no. 101, pp. 3-38; no. 152, pp. 1-51. Summary figures for the 1890 membership in the Evangelical, Lutheran, and Roman Catholic Churches of Wisconsin can be found in these pages, along with useful information regarding the official language in use by the various synods and congregations. In addition, see *Hoffman's Catholic Directory* (Milwaukee, 1889), pp. 87, 261, 284; *Catholic Statistics for Wisconsin, 1891* (n. p., 1891) [pamphlet in possession of the Wisconsin Historical Society], 4 pp.; and G.B. Schley, "Compulsory Education in Wisconsin: The Bennett Law," in *The Nation*, L (March 15, 1890), 240-241. Unfortunately, there is a slight variance between the different sources with regard to membership in the Catholic Church. Schley puts the number at 350,000; the *Catholic Directory*, at 325,000; and the U.S. Census Bureau at 249,164. For the purposes of this paper, the author has deemed it advisable to use the figure nearest the median of these three, particularly since this was the one provided by the official Roman *Catholic Directory*. A similar discrepancy, moreover, exists among the various sources for Lutheran membership totals for Wisconsin. Christian Koerner, in a list compiled from figures

The importance of these statistics can be even better understood after an examination of the pattern of German settlement in Wisconsin, as well as the problems contributing to the decision to emigrate to the new world. Contrary to general opinion, the main body of Wisconsin's German immigrants was not composed of political refugees from the unsuccessful German Revolution of 1848. This liberal and highly educated group, of whom Carl Schurz is perhaps the best known, formed but a comparatively small number of individuals, chiefly located in the cities and particularly the highly cosmopolitan center of Milwaukee. Consequently, although as members of the free-thinking Turnvereins they generally supported the Bennett measure, they had on the whole only minor influence over the farm settlers who comprised the bulk of Wisconsin's German-born population.[37]

The earliest of these settlers had been victims not of political but of religious persecution brought on by their own stubbornly conservative resistance to the scheme proposed in 1817 by the King of Prussia to unite all Lutheran and Reformed (Calvinist) congregations in his realm into a single State Church. Lutheran ministers and lay leaders such as Pastor Johannes A. Grabau (one of the later founders of the Buffalo Synod in America) and Captain Henry Von Rohr refused to allow any union with the Reformed group, whom they differed with in points of doctrine and suspected because of their emphasis on pietism.

---

submitted by teachers and pastors and published as an appendix to his *The Bennett law and German Parochial Schools of Wisconsin*, pp. 20-28, recorded a total of 127,038 members within the various German Lutheran and German Evangelical Synods in the state.

37 Louise Phelps Kellogg, "The Bennett Law in Wisconsin," *Wisconsin Magazine of History*, II (September, 1918), 7.

But opposition brought harassment in the form of fines and imprisonment, and it was not long before it seemed to them expedient to seek a new country where one's religious beliefs were not subject to dictation. To this end, Grabau and other recalcitrant ministers arranged and conducted the exodus of their congregations to the New World, where many of them settled as closely united, religiously oriented colonies on Wisconsin's fertile public lands. Even after actual persecution had been halted in Germany, numerous church groups, again led by their pastors, having heard of the richness of the new land, continued to emigrate to Wisconsin. Here they built communities similar to those they had known in Germany, where the church and the school served to perpetuate not only their former language but also the Old-World customs, traditions, and modes of thought.[38] Moreover, there was practically no opportunity for gradual modification of these traditions through casual contact with native American citizens, for as one contemporary writer remarked, these immigrants were "like the Puritans of old" who "built their churches on the hills" and as a result of their own zeal and "solidity of immigration" dominated the surrounding regions.[39]

Indeed, "solidity" was a fundamental characteristic of the distribution of Wisconsin's German population during this period of its history. In 1880, for example, Census data showed that most German-Americans were living in counties fronting on Lake Michigan and those immediately adjacent to them, while a

---

38 William F. Whyte, "The Settlement of Lebanon, Dodge County," in Wis. Hist. Soc. *Proceedings, 1915* (Madison, 1915), pp. 99-110. See also Kate Everest Levi, "The Geographical Origins of German Immigration to Wisconsin," in Wis. Hist. Soc. *Collections*, XIV (Madison, 1898), 341-363.
39 John Bascom, "A New Policy for the Public Schools," in *Forum*, XI (March 1891), 59-66 (esp. 66).

short northward arc of the population extended into Shawano, Marathon, and Lincoln counties.[40] In fact, so numerous were they in this Lakeshore region that the city of Milwaukee, where German immigrants and their children constituted 53.5 percent of the total population, became known as the "German Athens" of the New World.[41]

But if an understanding of a noticeable "clannishness" among the Germans can be gained from the fact that they faced a common oppression in their homeland and, once in America, tended to settle in closely knit communities headed by their pastors, a further insight into the matter can be discovered from a survey of the regions in Germany from which they originally came. Such a study was actually made in 1883, and from this it is clear that the main body of these immigrants, primarily the Lutherans, originated from North Germany and from the Prussian provinces of Pomerania, Posen, and West Prussia—i.e., from the heartland of German Junkerdom.[42] There as feudal farm laborers and village handicraftsmen under the domination

---

40 Kate A. Everest, "How Wisconsin Came by Its Large German Element," in Wis. Hist. Soc. *Collections*, XII (Madison, 1892), 298-334; map showing location of German settlers in the state according to the 1880 census, p. 304 f. For other maps of interest, see Kate Everest Levi, "Geographical Origins, etc.," p. 340 f. Dividing the total state German population into North Germans, South Germans, and Mixed, it plots their geographical distribution in Wisconsin according to the later census of 1890.
41 Kate A. Everest, "How Wisconsin etc.," p. 323. The *Eleventh Census of the U.S.: 1890. Population*, I, pp. 708-712, shows 109,278 German-born and children of German-born parents out of a total city population of 204,468. Moreover, if the number of foreign and native born with only one German parent were included in the total, the proportion of those in the city with some German ancestry would be raised to nearly 60 percent. See also Table 2, pp. 574-575 in Bayrd Still, *Milwaukee. The History of a City* (Madison, 1965). As a single group, the number of German-born residents of the city in 1890 represented 26.7 percent of the entire population.
42 Prussian citizens from the militaristic landowning class.

of the hereditary nobility, they had long been accustomed to subordination to both the state and the church. Thus, it is not difficult to understand why, when religious persecution drove them from their homeland and immigration delivered them from their feudal masters, they clung all the more tenaciously to the leadership of their clergymen, who had brought them safely to their new homes.[43]

The South Germans, on the other hand, were mainly Catholics, their work experience had encompassed more urban manufacturing, and their settlements in Wisconsin were more dispersed (e.g., in Sauk, Buffalo, Jefferson, and Ozaukee counties), thus allowing for greater personal contact with the English-speaking population. Nevertheless, their religious leaders, including Archbishop John Henni of Milwaukee (the first of his nationality to attain that office in the United States) and the bishops of Green Bay and La Crosse dioceses, were all German-born and German-educated.[44] Thus, like the Lutherans, they tended to cherish their homeland ties and center their hopes for the future in their parochial schools and churches.

With all this in mind, it is not at all surprising that the attitude of many of these settlers can be summed up in the statement of one who wrote: "The average German did not come to the United States to be Americanized."[45] On the contrary, during the Bennett Law controversy as well as before, there were occasions when the hope was expressed that the Germans would remain a distinct, if not superior, class in the population of the United States. Plans were

---

43 Kate Everest Levi, "Geographical Origins," pp. 341-367. See also Kellogg, "The Bennett Law," pp. 8-9.
44 Levi, pp. 367-391; Kellogg, p. 10. See also Benjamin J. Blied, *Three Archbishops of Milwaukee* (Milwaukee, 1955).
45 *Milwaukee Sentinel*, August 8, 1889, p. 4.

actually made in the 1830s and 1840s to create a separate German state in America, and as late as 1878, a German writer had strongly suggested that Wisconsin was ideally suited to this purpose.[46]

Further reflecting these feelings, during the Bennett Law agitation, the words "Germandom" and "Germanism" became commonplace.[47] Moreover, on numerous occasions, including the German-American Day celebrated throughout the state on October 6, 1890, in the midst of the all-important election campaign, attention was drawn to the many contributions German-Americans had made to the success of the American Revolution and Civil War.[48] A sense of nationalistic exclusiveness and extreme pride in their cultural heritage was manifested in their public stance and their relationship with the other citizens of their communities.

Quite naturally, perhaps, some of this attitude was carried over into their religious activities. Among the Lutherans, for example, there was a feeling, attested to by the Reverend G. H. Gerberding, one of the early founders of the English Evangelical Lutheran Synod of the Northwest, that worship in the English language

---

46   Kate A. Everest, "How Wisconsin etc.," pp. 303-310. One contemporary wrote of a convention held at Watertown in 1851 for the promotion and planning of such a German state. See William F. Whyte, "The Bennett Law Campaign in Wisconsin," *Wis. Mag. of Hist.*, X (1927), 364.

47   The *Reformer*, a German labor paper cited in the *Milwaukee Sentinel*, October 25, 1889, p. 4, stated: "The Germanists or German Know-nothings must not be permitted to form a state within a state.... A man may be both a German and a good American citizen, but can he be a good American citizen and a Germanist?" See also Kellogg, pp. 9, 12.

48   The *Milwaukee Sentinel*, on October 6-7, 1890, devoted much space to the German-American Day celebrated in that city and other parts of the state. Both Peck and Hoard, candidates for the governorship, spoke to the crowds which gathered to see the huge floats depicting the first settlement at Germantown, Pennsylvania, and the heroic deeds of DeKalb, Herkimer, Muhlenberg, and other German Revolutionary War figures. Twelve thousand marchers filled the streets. See also Still, pp. 261-262.

would spell an end to the true and necessary spirit of Lutheranism. It was, as he relates, "a well-settled tradition in the foreign synods and churches that when mother tongue was given up, mother Church must be sacrificed." Thus, when one young preacher had spoken English to a German audience, he was shouted down with the words, "*Unser Herr Gott ist ein deutscher Gott!* Our God is a *German* God!" And when a Milwaukee German told a friend that his neighbor, the Secretary of the English Lutheran Synod, was an Englishman, the amazed reply was: "Ach, no! . . . A preacher? A Lutheran? English? Ach, no! Dat it don't gif!"[49]

But the prevalence of such an attitude among the German element of both the Lutheran and Catholic Churches in Wisconsin, or indeed in any other state where a sizeable German-speaking population existed, also gave rise to some opposition by other church members who were not as hesitant about becoming part of their American communities, even if it meant sacrificing some of their Old-World traditions. It was this basic lack of unanimity that was rather caustically noted by leaders of the Bennett Law cause, when they demanded to know why only the *German* Catholics and *German* Lutherans could detect a threat to religious liberty from the state while their brethren of different nationalities generally favored such a statute.

Within the Lutheran Church, for example, the Scandinavian communicants were often found to support the principle of the law, even when their dislike of the district clause made them seek amendments to it. A Lutheran historian notes that the early Swedish settlers were quick to adapt to American ways, and unlike

---

49   The Reverend G.H. Gerberding, "Reminiscent Pioneering and Moralizing," in *Historical and Reminiscent Sketches: English Evangelical Lutheran Synod of the Northwest, 1891-1916* (n.p., 1916), pp. 38-40.

the Germans, were reluctant to support a separate parochial school system because this "did not seem 'American'" and they did not wish "to be considered 'foreigners.'"[50]

One such individual, the Reverend J. D. Nelsenius of the Ashland Swedish Lutheran Church, showed this attitude when he objected during the controversy to the inclusion of *all* Lutherans under one heading as opponents of the law. There were many in the church, he said, who like him supported the Bennett Law (with the exception of the district clause). "I think the Germans are going too far in their demands," he declared.[51]

Similar views were expressed by other Scandinavians during the campaign battle. Olaf Anderson, for example, chose to speak for his countrymen in Milwaukee and the state, when he announced that they would demonstrate their loyalty to their new land at the polls. "The Scandinavian becomes an American when he reaches the United States and he sees that his children are educated in the language of his adopted country. The Bennett Law is a good law and it should not be repealed or modified." A like sentiment was expressed by Theodore Saveland, who drew attention as well to the catastrophe suffered by the state when 50,000 children were left to languish in dingy factories and shops instead of acquiring at school the necessary skills for advancement in life. He believed strongly that "each and every child in this blessed country should be able to speak, read, and write in the English language, and it is eminently proper for the State to see to it that each child receives such an education."[52] The beliefs of both these men were shared by the Norwegian Lutherans of Vernon County who not

---
50 Oscar N. Olson, *The Augustana Lutheran Church in America, 1860-1910: The Formative Period* (Davenport, Iowa), 1956, p. 52.
51 *Milwaukee Sentinel*, September 5, 1890, p. 1.
52 *Milwaukee Sentinel*, March 28, 1890, p. 4.

only endorsed Governor Hoard by name, but also predicted his overwhelming victory in the November, 1890 election.[53]

However, if many Scandinavian Lutherans disagreed with their German brethren about the beneficence, or at least the harmlessness, of the Bennett Law, the same could be said regarding the attitudes of the German and Irish Catholics toward one another. The tenacity with which the German immigrants clung to their language and traditions, and the way in which they construed the English language clause to be an open threat to their religion, is nowhere more apparent than in a lengthy unsigned letter to the editor, published in the Catholic *Excelsior* on February 20, 1890.

At the very beginning of this message was printed a German patriotic poem, which had once roused that country to arms in an earlier day: "*Hab trischen Muth/ Du Deutsches Blut;/ Auf Gott vertraue!/ Und-um dich haue!*" ("O German blood/ Good courage show;/ Put trust in God!/ And smite the foe!") To the author of the letter, those words were not in the least inappropriate to the situation in Wisconsin, for he believed that a war had been kindled against the German-American, a war by cowards who chose to strike not directly at him but rather at his "inalienable heritage"—his language and religion.

> It is a simple fact that with the German, faith is closely allied to the German language. If now it is the design to take from your children their mother-tongue, then this is explained by their desire to quickly estrange your children from religion. This is the true object of the Bennett law.

In these and subsequent lines, the full magnitude of the German writer's desire to preserve his racial and religious exclusiveness

---
[53] *Milwaukee Sentinel*, September 25, 1890, p. 1.

became apparent. Indeed, throughout the letter nothing was more evident than its appeal to national pride. State officials who had enacted the Bennett Law were branded "despots" acting "in a true Russian knout style," and it was said of them:

> They intend to take away from you, noble German (you, who, though poor, helped to convert the clods of this fair land into tillable acres), your heritage, your language!
>
> They intend to forbid you, brave German (you, who brandished the sword for the starry banner), your noblest treasure on earth, your melodious mother tongue!
>
> They wish to (and that is the most important)—they want to, self-sacrificing German! (you, who with the labor of your hands, and your sweat, built churches for your children, in order to preserve your best goods, your religion and your mother-tongue)—they want to subjugate you now! They want to make you the slave of others. . . . And a slave you become, German, if you let yourself be robbed by a flagitious hand of your language, and with it, your religion!

The remedy, however, was in their grasp, if they chose to exercise it. Thus, once more the poetic call to arms was given, and readers were urged to use the ballot as a weapon to "smite the foe!"[54]

These militant and rather chauvinistic sentiments illuminate a dispute that was taking place in the Catholic Church at about the same time the Bennett Law discussion was filling the newspaper pages in Wisconsin. This was a dispute that centered on the problem of whether or not to allow the erection in the United States of national parishes, each headed by a priest native to the country from which his parishioners came. It is important to

---

54 *Milwaukee Excelsior*, February 20, 1890, p. 4. English translation in *Bennett Law Clippings*, I (scrapbook in the possession of the Wis. Hist. Soc.), 26-27.

draw attention to the fact that these two issues, the Bennett Law controversy and the Cahenslyism movement, as the latter came to be called, although apparently separate questions, were merely different manifestations of an all-encompassing problem faced by all immigrant churches at this time—i.e., the need for accommodation of the church to the New-World situation. Indeed, the Reverend Colman J. Barry has written that "it was the school question, coming to the front in 1890, which united the cause of the 'Cahenslyites' with other non-Germans and extended the life of the nationality question long beyond what at first seemed to be a final decision in the matter, when Cardinal Rampolla conveyed the opinion of Leo XIII to Cardinal Gibbons on June 28, 1891."[55]

A short examination of the early history of the Cahensly movement as manifested in Wisconsin, as well as the role of the Irish in the Americanization issue, is therefore in order. As we have seen, the Germans in Wisconsin were determined to maintain their language intact, and for this reason the suggestion of national parishes, headed by German bishops, was definitely appealing. Articles therefore began appearing in numerous German Catholic papers endorsing a report by Archbishop Francis A. Janssens of New Orleans on the condition of the missions of his diocese, where French was giving way to English, and similar Catholic statements—all attesting to the belief that members of the different nationalities in the United States must receive their religious instruction in their mother tongue or lose, along with their language, their religious convictions.[56]

---

55 Colman J. Barry, *The Catholic Church and German Americans* in Catholic University of America *Studies*, 40 (Washington, D.C., 1953), 184.
56 Reprinted in *Milwaukee Sentinel*, November 25, 1889, p. 4; February 22, 1890, p. 4.

This opinion was carried to Rome in 1886 by Father Peter M. Abbelen of Milwaukee, with the consent and approval of Archbishop Michael Heiss, as a preview of the more famous St. Raphaelsverein Protest, or Cahensly petition, of 1891. Father Abbelen, who had himself emigrated from Germany in 1886 and who now served as spiritual director for the School Sisters of Notre Dame in Milwaukee, was convinced that German Catholics in general were in danger of becoming second-class members of the church. To remedy this situation, he hoped that an implementation of the suggested national parishes could soon be effected by the Propaganda at Rome.[57]

Nevertheless, he reckoned without the opposition of the Irish, whose position on the question can be inferred from the title of Abbelen's petition: "The question in the United States between the German Catholics and the Irish Catholics." Indeed, throughout both the Cahensly movement and the Bennett Law controversy, it was the Irish (like the Scandinavians among the Lutherans) who advocated the accommodation of their church to the new American social climate. As an English-speaking group, they saw little to fear from this move and, therefore, as one modern religious sociologist has written, were already serving as a necessary catalyst by which the Catholic Church in America would gradually be reshaped into an "American religious community."[58]

Unfortunately for the German cause and Abbelen's secret petition, two Irish-American bishops who were in attendance at

---

57 John Tracy Ellis, *The Life of James Cardinal Gibbons, Archbishop of Baltimore, 1834-1921*, I (Milwaukee, 1952), pp. 347-383; Blied, pp. 38-41, 61. For an unfriendly view of the proposed plan for national parishes by a Wisconsin Catholic, see a letter to the editor, signed "Catholicity," in the *Milwaukee Sentinel*, April 16, 1890, p. 3.
58 Herberg, p. 147.

Rome at this time—Bishop John Ireland of St. Paul and Bishop John J. Keane of Richmond—learned of the proposal and were quick to mount opposition to it, declaring that the real question at issue involved whether or not a party would be allowed to perpetuate itself within the Catholic Church, which based its claims to distinction on the single fact that its members spoke a language different from that of the country in which they lived. The only answer these bishops could conceive, in view of the very heterogeneous population of the United States, was that the Catholic Church must direct its efforts toward unifying and nationalizing its communion in the major language of the country, while resisting the divisions engendered in the consciousness of a foreign heritage.[59]

As a result of these forcefully written statements, as well as the letters of support that were delivered to the Propaganda from other American bishops, Father Abbelen's petition was a failure. But the debate between Irish Catholics and German Catholics did not abate during this period. Governor Hoard, himself, noted this division in several of his personal letters, and, notwithstanding the fact that many were originally Democrats, he expected to gain considerable support from the Irish during the November election. Numerous Irish-Americans corresponded with the governor to express their intentions of supporting him, as did several priests like the Reverend Daniel B. Toomery, who wrote that no "Bishop, Priest, or Minister who is a true American and has the best interests of America at heart as well as those under his care, can be so far forgetful of his duty to the country as to try to supplant the language of his adopted country with one he

---

59 *Milwaukee Sentinel*, April 16, 1890, p. 3; Ellis, *Gibbons*, pp. 349-351.

has abjured."[60] Other Irish clergymen were equally clear in their support of the law, including the Reverend Hickey of Springfield, Illinois, Archbishop John Ireland of St. Paul, his assistant Bishop James McGolrick, and Father Hannon of Fond du Lac.[61]

But opposition was not confined to the clergy. It was often noted, for example, that Michael John Bennett himself, who introduced and afterward defended the law, was an Irishman and a Catholic and had seen no danger to his church or its parochial schools from the proposal. John Nagle, influential editor of the *Manitowoc Pilot*, an Irishman and former Democrat, also proved to be an outspoken advocate of the measure during the controversy. Another was Jeremiah Quinn, a prominent Milwaukee Catholic, who wrote numerous letters to the editor of the *Milwaukee Sentinel* in which he declared that the real danger to parental rights arose not from the Bennett Law but from priests and bishops who used the threat of eternal punishment and refusal of church rites to attack those Catholics who sent their children to public, rather than parochial, schools.[62] Thomas Kelly of Fond du Lac agreed with this view and declared that he could not in conscience "follow the directions of German bishops. When they begin to dabble with politics and direct my vote, they are out of their province and I will not hear them."[63]

Thus, throughout the months of 1889 and 1890, the Bennett Law discussion and the more universal Cahensly issue proceeded

---

60 Hoard, *Private Letter Books*, 17:301-302.
61 *Milwaukee Sentinel*, March 22, 1890, p. 4; April 23, p. 4. *Milwaukee Daily Journal*, April 18, 1890, p. 1; *Fond du Lac Commonwealth*, February 14, 1890. Father De Kelver of Menasha, a native Wisconsinite of Belgian ancestry, also joined with many of the Irish clergy in supporting the law. *Milwaukee Sentinel*, February 27, 1890, p. 4; *Fond du Lac Commonwealth*, October 24, 1890.
62 *Milwaukee Sentinel*, October 21, 1890, p. 5; *Chicago Tribune*, April 10, 1890, p. 4.
63 *Milwaukee Sentinel*, April 26, 1890, p. 4. See also *Fond du Lac Commonwealth*, April 11, 1890.

apace together. In general, those who supported one opposed the other, and in the center was the overriding question of whether Americanization would be allowed to progress naturally within the church. Archbishop Ireland spoke for believers in this course when he remarked to the Wisconsin Governor at a reception in St. Paul:

> Governor Hoard, you must stand up, I must stand up. All who believe in America and Americanism must stand up and fight this poisonous spirit of foreignism.[64]

German Catholics, on the other hand, continued to urge their followers to resist the same spread of Americanism for God and for Fatherland. As a result of such opposition, the Bennett Law was repealed in February, 1891, but the victory was short-lived, for several months later Pope Leo XIII's apostolic letter to Cardinal Gibbons in reply to the St. Raphaelsverein Protest (the Cahensly petition) dashed all hope for national parishes and national bishops.[65] More importantly, as Rasmus B. Anderson, an influential Lutheran opponent of the law, once predicted, the English language continued to stride through the land "in seven league boots" so that gradually, despite ever-vigilant opposition to legislative measures such as the one under discussion, the Catholic Church, like all immigrant churches, found that the process of Americanization could not be halted. In the next generation, English became commonplace and the church itself an American institution.

It is with this understanding that the following discussion of the Bennett Law must be read. The controversy surrounding its

---

64 Quoted in Rankin, p. 134.
65 John Tracy Ellis, ed., *Documents of American Catholic History* (Milwaukee, 1962), pp. 476-479 ("St. Raphaelsverein Protest"). See also *Wisconsin State Journal*, July 1, 1891, p. 1, for the reply of Pope Leo XIII.

passage and ultimate repeal did, indeed, involve the question of church-state relations. In the minds of most opponents of the law, state paternalism, parental rights, and liberty of conscience were the chief points at issue. Yet, unlike the Oregon case of 1925, the Wisconsin debate contained another element of dissension that made its nature more complex than those that followed it. This was the futile but quite vigorous resistance of numerous foreign-born citizens to any practical accommodation to the new land in their language, customs, or religious traditions.

The Anti-Bennett Law Campaign Begins

The first slight intimation of the great flood of opposition that was to come occurred in June, 1889, two months after the Bennett proposal had been signed into law. At that time, two German synods meeting at Portage and Sheboygan, whose combined membership totaled 62,904, denounced the educational law as an attack upon German churches, schools, language, and the press.[66] Thereafter, religious opposition to the law grew steadily.

The Evangelical Lutheran Synod of Wisconsin, while sitting at Milwaukee from June 20 to 25, passed resolutions specifically attacking the enactment as "tyrannical and unjust." Its enforcement, they insisted, would not only rob parents of their right to send their children to a school of their own choice, but would also threaten the very existence of the Synod's churches and parochial schools. Thus, the members of that synod, a total of

---

66 *Milwaukee Journal*, June 15-18, 1889, p. 1; June 24, p. 1. Membership statistics for the Wisconsin district of the Missouri Synod, which met at Sheboygan, and the Evangelical Synod, which met at Portage, were derived from figures given in Koerner, *The Bennett Law*, p. 26 (Appendix).

46,375 German Lutherans, went on record in demanding repeal of the measure or its suitable amendment and declared that unless their demands were heeded, further action in the courts or at the ballot box would follow. A statement along similar lines was issued soon after by the Wisconsin District of the Missouri Synod, representing some 54,032 German Lutherans.

Both of these groups appointed steering committees in order to interview potential political candidates as to their stand on the law, to aid parents who were fined or prosecuted under its provisions, and to publish articles on the progress of their opposition. Eventually, these two committees united and began a joint campaign, which was supplemented by the work of other Lutheran church committees associated with individual congregations.[67]

Nevertheless, it is a surprising fact that for a rather long time politicians of both political parties evaded the issue. The *Milwaukee Sentinel* had introduced the Bennett Law question to the people at large when in early July it published a series of articles by Henry E. Legler, one of its reporters, on the condition of Lutheran parochial schools in Milwaukee.[68] The Democrats, however, far from taking an early stand on the measure seemed to want to bide their time, waiting to see how forceful the opposition became before committing themselves. Thus, two of their most prominent party organs, the *Madison Daily Democrat* and the *Milwaukee Journal*, devoted but little space to the problem

---

67 *Milwaukee Journal*, June 24, 1889, p. 1; Stellhorn, pp. 238-243. Membership statistics from Koerner, p. 26 (Appendix).
68 *Milwaukee Sentinel*, July 1,2,3,7,8, 1889. These articles reported that in Milwaukee, at least, most Lutheran parochial schools taught some English and were thus within the letter of the law, which required only twelve weeks each year of such teaching.

during the summer and fall of 1889, and leading Democratic politicians wavered between lukewarm support of the law, which they felt was unenforceable anyway, to hesitant opposition. The prevailing view, however, seemed to be that the measure would not become an issue in the next campaign. J. E. Dodge, a member of the Democratic State Central Committee, said for example: "I do not believe that the Bennett law is worthy of a position as an issue in state politics. It is an insignificant measure, and contains nothing new except an unnecessary interference with private rights which I believe should be removed. There are more important issues for the democratic party."[69]

For Governor Hoard, however, there was no more important problem confronting the state than the inability of many American-born children even to speak the language of their own country. In his many speeches and public statements, as well as in his confidential letters to both friends and critics during the controversy, it is clear that the governor thought of this matter as one of principle, involving not only the right of a child to an adequate education but also the duty of the state to require a sound basis for civic responsibility.

To William Cramer, editor of the *Milwaukee Evening Wisconsin*, he wrote for example that the coming campaign would be one "of principles *not men*." It would be "a contest on behalf of the little children of the State, involving the question of good citizenship," and was far "more important to the people of the state than the political advancement of any individual."[70] At another time, speaking at a county fair in Medford, Wisconsin,

---

69 *Milwaukee Journal*, April 4, 1890, p. 4. See also *Madison Daily Democrat*, January 11, 1890, p. 2; April 5, p. 1.
70 Hoard, *Private Letter Books*, 16:219.

before an audience composed primarily of German-Americans, the governor expressed deep concern for the future of the state's young people. "The little German boy, the little Polish boy, the little Scandinavian boy, and the little Bohemian boy, all have the right to be allowed to learn the English language, the language of the country of which they are natives. They are young Americans and they must have as good a show as the other little natives who happened to be born of English-speaking parents."[71]

Such solicitude for what critics of the law henceforth sarcastically referred to as "the poor little German boy" was bitterly resented by German parents, who believed they were the best judge of what constituted the welfare of their own children. Some pointed to prominent German-Americans in law, politics, and education as proof that the parochial and public school systems needed no further improvements in the manner proposed by the Bennett Law.[72] At a later date, it was even suggested that Hoard might have hoped to use the issue as a stepping stone to the presidency, an allegation that was vehemently denied by the governor, who insisted throughout that his single concern was that the youth of the state be properly equipped to take their places in adult society.[73]

At this point, a word should be said regarding the position and attitude of Governor Hoard in the controversy. Even a cursory, unbiased reading of his many letters and public statements throughout the debate reveals a sincerity as deep as any

---

71 *Milwaukee Journal*, October 21, 1889, p. 1.
72 *Milwaukee Journal*, October 3, 1890, p. 4. See also Koerner, *The Bennett Law*.
73 Anderson, *Life Story*, p. 595. See also Governor Hoard's letter of reply in Appendix, pp. 672-75. A similar statement of denial by the governor was made in an interview with Dr. Louise Phelps Kellogg. See her notes, p. 4, in Kellogg Papers.

manifested by religious opponents of the law. For the governor, the entire problem was, indeed, one of principle, and despite the admonitions of more cautious professional politicians, he was quite prepared to fall, if need be, on that issue. Nevertheless, he stubbornly maintained that in the end the good sense of his religious opponents would prevail and they would come to feel, as he did, that the principle of the law was a right one "for the welfare of the child, of the parent, of the state, of the nation, and of civilization in general."[74]

So strong was his faith in the ability of all voters to make the right decision in the matter that he refused to condone the printing and distribution of any anti-Catholic or nativist material in the state, as some less scrupulous advisers suggested, on the grounds that the Catholic Church contained as large a number of patriotic citizens as any other.[75] Furthermore, he insisted that he was opposed neither to the Germans as a people nor to their language. In fact, as he proudly pointed out, his own grandmother was German, and he himself had not only been responsible for adding the German language to the curriculum of Fort Atkinson public schools, but for a time had paid for such instruction out of his own pocket.[76]

Moreover, his own views on the necessity of a knowledge of English by all Americans had stemmed mainly from an early misfortune experienced by a number of immigrant farm families in Wisconsin. As a census taker for four strongly German townships in 1870, Hoard soon discovered that three swindlers who spoke German fluently had preceded him, convinced the non-English-

---

74 Interview in the *Milwaukee Journal*, May 5, 1890, p. 1.
75 Hoard, *Private Letter Books*, 17:107.
76 *Ibid.*, 17:365; 18: 204-205.

speaking farmers that they were official census takers, and as a result had succeeded in obtaining their signatures on documents that were in reality promissory notes worth $8,000. When Hoard himself arrived to fulfill his duties, the angry townspeople confronted him, and he was forced to tell them that their money had been stolen. Yet their predicament, he was convinced, could easily have been avoided if they had had even a rudimentary knowledge of the language in which the laws and official transactions of government were written.[77]

Nonetheless, as governor, his sincerity in the matter was not sufficiently clear to the parties who made up the opposition. As the year 1889 ended, anti-Bennett Law agitation began to develop more strength and a wider hearing. Thus, on December 27, 1889, a meeting at the home of Pastor John Bading of St. John's Evangelical Lutheran Church in Milwaukee attracted some fifty representatives from the German Lutheran congregations of Wisconsin and several German Catholic lay leaders.

Colonel Conrad Krez, of Sheboygan, addressed the group. A lawyer by profession, Krez had been born and educated in Germany, and his attachment to the fatherland had not ceased with his immigration to America in 1851. Indeed, his lyric poetry praising the German heritage was widely renowned among German-Americans even outside Wisconsin. During the Bennett Law controversy, however, his literary talent was turned to the writing of often comic campaign poetry, which was circulated throughout the state. Although not a church member, he attended many religious conferences during the debates, and his advice was accepted by the leading opponents of the law among the clergy. Critics, however, pointed out that Krez had been turned out of

---

[77] Rankin, p. 124.

his job as Customs Collector for the Port of Milwaukee in 1889 by the newly elected Republican President Benjamin Harrison and that his attitude toward the Bennett Law befitted a deposed Democratic officeholder.[78]

Now in his speech before representatives of both the German Lutheran and German Catholic Churches in Wisconsin, he began by hinting broadly that the public schools were the spawning ground for "loafers," and went on to denounce the Bennett Act as "tyrannical." It was his stated opinion that any German who could support such a law could only be looked upon as a "traitor to his mother tongue." As to the charge that overt opposition meant violation of state law, he retorted: "We want it to be understood that we are the state! We pay the officials, the governor, the legislature. . . . The Germans only want their rights as they have had them heretofore; if they suffer them to be taken away from them, then they are not worthy to speak the language of Luther, not worthy to be the brothers of those Germans who fought at

---

78 See, e.g., John R. Berryman, *History of the Bench and Bar of Wisconsin*, I (Chicago, 1898), 548. A sonnet attacking the Bennett Law is reprinted in the *Milwaukee Sentinel*, August 5, 1890, p. 4. Dr. William F. Whyte recalls one address at Watertown in which Krez compared German sauerkraut to a Yankee pumpkin pie, determining that the former was far superior to the pie. See Whyte, "The Bennett Law Campaign," p. 383. In his best known poem, "An mein Vaterland" (1870), however, the full patriotic fervor of love for the homeland, felt so keenly by many German-Americans in Wisconsin, was expressed. The fourth stanza is especially indicative of the attitude that manifested itself in an intense opposition to any proposal which, like the Bennett Law, seemed to threaten their beloved national heritage.

Land of my fathers! Though no longer mine,
If any soil is sacred, it is thine;
Thy image, always bright, is in my mind,
And if no tie were wrought by living hand,
My cherished dead would me to thee still bind,
Thy holy graves—O thou, my Fatherland.

Translated by Robert Wild in Ellis B. Usher, *Wisconsin, Its Story and Biography, 1848-1913*, IV (Chicago and New York, 1914), 644.

Mars-la-Tour. But they will only be heeded if they are feared!" In short, to prevent "the forcible extinction of the German language," voters had to be organized and an all-out campaign for repeal of the hated law begun.[79]

Though denounced in the *Manitowoc Pilot* as "inverted know-nothingism," this speech clearly represented the feelings and determination of those German-Americans to whom Krez was speaking. At the same meeting, a State Central Committee of fifteen men was appointed and instructed to write a platform and draw up plans for the coming election campaign, which would then be presented at an anti-Bennett Law convention to be held in June, 1890. In addition, a joint statement of resolutions was drawn up and approved by both the Lutheran and Catholic delegates to the meeting. It declared the law to be "unrepublican," "unconstitutional," and destructive to parental authority, and therefore called upon those present, without reference to party, to oppose all candidates who supported the law and to actively campaign for the election of those pledged to its repeal.[80]

Colonel Krez had proclaimed the Bennett measure "a war on Germans," and it was at this fateful meeting that the German-Americans of both the Catholic and Protestant faiths closed ranks against what they believed to be an unjust attack upon their language and religion. Governor Hoard remarked that "the Bennett law had done what the devil had tried to do for three

---

79 *Milwaukee Journal*, December 28, 1889, p. 1. *Milwaukee Sentinel*, December 30, 1889, p. 4 (translation of Colonel Krez's speech first published in *The Herold*; December 31, p. 4 (letter from Colonel Krez defending his remarks). See also similar statements by Colonel Krez in *Wisconsin State Journal*, October 29, 1890, p. 8.

80 *Manitowoc Pilot*, January 2, 1890, in *Bennett Law Clippings*, I, 67. *Milwaukee Sentinel*, January 6, 1890, p. 8.

hundred years and had failed to accomplish, namely to unite the Lutherans and Catholics."[81]

In an attempt to allay some of this concern and to explain the law in detail, State Superintendent of Schools Jesse B. Thayer first issued an open letter to the people and then a directive to school district boards, outlining the meaning of each provision of the statute, the benefits to be derived from it, and the ways in which the right of conscience and parental authority were safeguarded.[82] Nevertheless, this action was of little consequence, for less than a week later on January 31, 1890, the Reverend Killian Flasch, Bishop of the La Crosse diocese, spoke out in opposition to the law. It was the first time that a Catholic priest had made a public statement on the Bennett Law issue, and it was considered by many to be a sign to the other priests in the state that open opposition was now in order. Significantly, he denounced the statute for opposing not only his church but his Mother Country, as well.[83]

The following month, on February 27, 1890, representatives from all the German Protestant churches of Milwaukee met in convention to determine their stand on the Bennett Law question. In action similar to that of the earlier meeting in December, a lengthy statement was soon issued which declared that because the law was for them "in direct opposition to the personal liberty of conscience" guaranteed by both the national and state constitutions and interfered with the parent's authority over his own child, they could do nothing but oppose the law by all

---

81 Kellogg, "Interview Notes," p. 3. See also Anderson, *Life Story*, p. 595.
82 *Milwaukee Journal*, December 20, 1889, p. 1. J.B. Thayer, *Circular from the Office of State Superintendent of Schools to School Directors, etc.*, January 25, 1890, 3 pp. [Copy preserved in *Bound Bennett Law Pamphlets*, Wis. Historical Society.]
83 *Bennett Law Clippings*, I, 12.

legal means and seek to have it repealed at the next session of the legislature. To this end, the delegation set up a central anti-Bennett Law committee which would send out circulars to all candidates in Milwaukee's upcoming city election in order to determine their stand on the issue. Members of the churches represented at the meeting were pledged to vote only for candidates who signified their determination to repeal the law.[84]

With the formation of smaller anti-Bennett Law clubs attached to Lutheran churches throughout the city and the open declaration by the Catholic Church that it was unalterably opposed to the measure, the stage was now set for a flurry of public pronouncements by religious and political leaders alike. The case for the state was given by the Milwaukee City Attorney, Eugene S. Elliott, in a public reply to the members of the committee of German Protestant churches, which had just met. He denied that the law sought in any way to interfere with private denominational schools, but insisted that the public school system was the basis for all other American institutions and as such was in need of protection and support. Furthermore, the English language was the "birthright" of each child in the state, and without it no individual could "properly discharge the duties" or "enjoy the advantages of American citizenship." Finally, he would point out that the evils of child labor were far too real to allow the repeal of an effective compulsory education law.[85]

A number of Lutheran ministers were equally vociferous, however, in declaring their reasons for denouncing the measure.

---

84   *Milwaukee Sentinel*, March 25, 1890, p. 4. *Declarations and Resolutions adopted by a meeting of representative laymen of the German protestant churches in Milwaukee, held Febr. 27th (1890)*...(Milwaukee, 1890), 2 pp. [Broadside in possession of the Wisconsin Historical Society.]
85   *Milwaukee Sentinel*, March 26, 1890, p. 4; March 27, p. 4.

Letters from clergymen in Burlington, Oshkosh, Jefferson, Racine, Janesville, Bay View, La Crosse, and other towns throughout the state, registered their disapproval and their determination to see that the law was eventually removed from the statute books. Though careful to voice their allegiance to the English language and the public schools, they insisted that the Bennett Law was "meddling with affairs that to a great part do not concern the state whatsoever." Throughout Wisconsin, Lutheran congregations followed the lead of their Milwaukee brethren in agreeing to make their feelings known in the next election.[86]

By this time, too, the state press began to take up the issue in earnest, and it became apparent that a strong division existed among them. Some Democratic organs found themselves supporting what had become a partisan Republican measure, and former Republican papers discovered that their interests now lay with their erstwhile political opponents. In general, the pro-Bennett Law papers denied that the question at issue was one involving encroachment of the state in church affairs. In their eyes the real problem involved the stubborn resistance of some Germans, particularly ministers and newspaper editors who had a vested interest in maintaining the German language, to any accommodation to the conditions of American society. Reflecting this view, the Appleton *Post* declared:

> The degree of selfishness manifested in the opposition to the Bennett Law is perfectly intolerable to every fair-minded citizen. It is nothing more nor less than virulent

---

86 *Milwaukee Sentinel*, February 18, 1890, p. 4; Feb. 23, p. 7; March 17, p. 2; March 18, p. 8; March 20, p. 1; April 9, p. 4; April 24, p. 4. *Madison Daily Democrat*, March 18, 1890, p. 1. *Milwaukee Daily Journal*, March 19, 1890, p. 2.

know-nothingism. It is a protest against teaching the language of the country to the children of the country that a few people engaged in certain professions may not lose their occupations.[87]

Similar views were proclaimed in the *Waukesha Freeman*, *Wausau Torch*, *Two Rivers Chronicle*, and other local journals. To these proponents of the new law, it was the clear right of the state to train its citizens for its own best interests, as well as the patriotic duty of all citizens to defend this prerogative. Said the editor of the *Marinette Eagle*: "It is not a question of either politics or religion, but a question of the protection of the rights of the state by extending such protection to the children who are to make its future citizens."[88]

To the anti-Bennett Law journals, however, particularly those printed in a foreign language or representing a religious interest, the issue was simply one of paternalism, or undue state interference with private rights and conscience. The *Columbia*, a Catholic organ published in Milwaukee, declared that it was the church, not the state that had received Christ's command to go into the world and teach, and almost all of the opposition papers made the preservation of parental authority a byword.[89]

Nevertheless, the question of maintaining the German language was never far from their thoughts. The *Milwaukee Seebote*, the *Manitowoc Nordwestern*, and the *Germania*, all charged that the secret purpose of the law, which had been passed by the "Anglo-Americans," was to prevent children of German parents from learning their mother tongue and, as a result, to "denationalize" them.

---

87 Reprinted in the *Milwaukee Sentinel*, March 8, 1890, p. 4.
88 *Ibid.* See also *Bennett Law Clippings*, I, 28, 36-39, 52-55.
89 Translated in the *Milwaukee Sentinel*, January 15, 1890, p. 4.

> To such people who will recognize as 'Americans' only those whose ancestors lived here during the war of the revolution [wrote the editor of the *Germania*], the German who clings to his home customs and to his glorious native tongue is an annoyance. It is not sufficient for them that we should become Americanized—we want them to do that in the proper manner, of course—but they want us to become de-Germanized. And they think that can be accomplished first by destroying German schools.

The Germans, the editor went on, asked only the right to regulate their own schools and to preserve their German character "as a bulwark of old German customs and as a bulwark of the German mother tongue." Against all "new-fangled laws" that interfered with this purpose they were determined to fight.[90]

As proof of this determination, on March 12, 1890, the most important Catholic pronouncement of the entire campaign was issued. This "Catholic Manifesto" or "Bishops' Protest," as it came to be known, was the result of the combined efforts of Bishop Frederick X. Katzer of Green Bay, Bishop Killian Flasch of La Crosse, and Archbishop Michael Heiss of Milwaukee, who believed it was now time for the position of the Catholic Church on the law to be explicitly and publicly stated. In their protest, they attempted to make it clear that their only objection to the law was its interference with the rights of the church and of parents and not its required teaching of English in parochial schools. The true aim of the law, they believed, was not to promote a greater knowledge of the language of the country among its citizens, but rather to forcibly bring their parochial schools under state control and ultimately to destroy their private school system completely.

---

90 Translated from the *Germania* in *Bennett Law Clippings*, I, 43. See also translation of Manitowoc *Nordwestern* in *Milwaukee Sentinel*, January 8, 1890, p. 4 and of the *Seebote* in *Milwaukee Sentinel*, January 6, 1890, p. 4.

For these and other reasons the law was deemed "unnecessary," "offensive," and "unjust."

It was unnecessary, the bishops were careful to point out, because English was taught in most of their parochial schools, and it certainly was offensive and outrageous to suggest that Catholic parents were incapable or uninterested in securing the most proper education for their own children. Above all, however, the law was unjust not only in its extreme penalties for noncompliance, but because of its intolerable interference with the "sacred, inalienable rights of parents." For it was, after all, a duty placed upon such individuals by their church to see to it that their children received a Christian education, encompassing not only secular instruction but religious training, as well. For this reason, the Catholic Church obliged parents to send their children to parochial schools. The Bennett Law, however, as interpreted by the priests, would interfere to an untenable degree with that right.

Section 1, for example, insisted that the child attend only those schools within his own district, and Section 5 gave the school boards power to determine what constituted a school under the law. Thus, reluctantly, the need for an open protest had been thrust upon them. "We want to live in peace and good fellowship with all our fellow citizens,'" wrote the three bishops. Nevertheless, "we have never received one single cent of State help for our schools," and "we want no State interference with them either."[91]

This manifesto was read in Catholic churches throughout Wisconsin and evoked widespread response from many quarters. As might be expected, Governor Hoard took exception to the protest and made a public statement concerning it. In his reply,

---

91 Harry H. Heming, *History of the Catholic Church in Wisconsin* (Milwaukee, 1896), pp. 281-287. See also the *Milwaukee Journal*, March 12, 1890, p. 1 and the *Milwaukee Sentinel*, March 13, 1890, p. 4.

the governor once more drew attention to the real necessity for some compulsory education law as he pointed out that one-twelfth of all school-age children residing in Wisconsin had not attended school for a single day in the past year. Surely, the state had a *duty* to remedy this situation and also a *right*, for "the power of compulsory education is inherent in the power of compulsory taxation for educational purposes."

It was unfair, moreover, to charge that the Bennett Law interfered with any church or parochial school system. Such private denominational schools had a strong constitutional basis for existence and no state law, including the present one, had ever been designed to interfere with their right of self-management. In point of fact, Governor Hoard argued, the state's only concern was with the parent who must be responsible for the proper education of his children. This and only this was the aim of the Bennett Law, which heretofore had been so completely misinterpreted and misunderstood. As a result, its defenders were being held up to the people as "'Nationalists,' 'Knownothings,' . . . hostile to the German people and the German language." Yet, their only concern had been "the unselfish desire that every child in the state, no matter what blood or nationality, shall have just as fair a chance for all the country has to confer in its future as the child of the bluest Yankee blood. If this be 'nativistic' or 'knownothingism'" said the governor, "then I don't know the meaning of the terms."[92]

At the unofficial level, the Milwaukee Turners, in keeping with their original support of the law, passed resolutions denouncing the manifesto as an unwarranted interference in political affairs.[93] But of even more importance, there was also at this time some

---

92 *Milwaukee Sentinel*, March 19, 1890, p. 4.
93 *Milwaukee Sentinel*, March 13, 1890, p. 1; March 14, p. 1; March 20, p. 1.

reaction to the protest within the Catholic Church itself. Most, of course, applauded the strong statement of their bishops, but enough misgivings were aired to suggest that many priests were seriously troubled about the advisability of rejecting a law that was basically concerned only with increasing school attendance and ensuring a rudimentary knowledge of English among all the inhabitants of the state. The Reverend John Gmeiner, himself a German and the head of the seminary of St. Francis, wrote in reply to the Bishops' Protest:

> I candidly believe that we German Catholics ought to accept thankfully from the hands of Providence the American surroundings in which we are placed, to conform ourselves to them as far as prudence and conscience may dictate, and not to expect it to be the mission of the Catholic Church to obstruct forcibly with her authority the natural course of events, in favor of any particular nationality or language, though this may happen to be our own.

The best course for the Catholic Church in this country, he believed, was to eschew the label of a foreign institution. It should become neither an Irish-American, a German-American, a Polish-American, or any other composite religious organization—but rather it should strive first of all and simply to be an *American* church. To promote this goal of union and harmony among the various nationalities, moreover, the English language would prove to be an invaluable aid.[94]

A similar view was taken by many Irish Catholics. In an open letter to the three Wisconsin bishops who criticized the Bennett Law, John Brennan expressed gratitude for the fact that the Church of Rome had been allowed to flourish and grow in a

---

94 *Milwaukee Sentinel*, March 17, 1890, p. 4.

predominantly Protestant state. Indeed, the idea of a plot for the gradual destruction of parochial schools by the state he dismissed as the mere "fairy creatures" of their imagination. To these bishops he thus remonstrated:

> If you would bring our people and our school children out of their environment of exclusiveness and co-mingle with the people of the state. . . , if you would cease your apprehensions and suspicions . . . , the strife and dissension that you mention in your protest need not be feared, and all the Catholics of Wisconsin could live as they do live, notwithstanding the blunders of a certain nationality, in peace and good fellowship with their fellow citizens.[95]

Finally, in addition to these general misgivings, the Polish Catholics also declared publicly their reluctance to accept the pronouncements of the German prelates. For example, at the St. Stanislaus Church in Milwaukee, where the manifesto was read from the pulpit along with a personal adjuration from the priest that those present actively protest against the law, the reaction was not at all what had been intended. Several members declared flatly that all Polish parochial schools were well within the law and therefore they not only favored the Bennett Act but anxiously prayed for its enforcement throughout the state. Furthermore, in their opinion, it was but a poor misrepresentation to depict the law as an attack upon their religion, schools, or mother tongue, which the perusal of any correct translation of the statute would soon reveal.[96] "I tell you Governor Hoard is right on this question," said one parochial school teacher, himself a recent immigrant, "and many Polanders, who can not be bullied by priests and democratic ward heelers, will vote for him too."[97]

---

95 *Milwaukee Sentinel*, March 31, 1890, p. 6.
96 *Milwaukee Sentinel*, March 15, 1890, p. 3; March 17, p. 2.
97 *Milwaukee Sentinel*, October 16, 1890, p. 2.

By coincidence, it was in the middle of this uproar over the Bishops' Manifesto that the Supreme Court of Wisconsin handed down a decision against Bible-reading in state-funded public schools. The original suit had been brought by a number of Roman Catholic families in Edgerton against the district school board for allowing the reading of the Bible (King James Version) in public schools. The Rock County circuit court had upheld the school board, but the decision had been subsequently appealed to the high court. Then, on March 19, 1890, these justices ruled that Bible-reading in the classroom was inconsistent with the clause in the state constitution which forbade "sectarian instruction" in public schools. Therefore, the Edgerton school board was directed by a writ of mandamus to see to it that such readings in the Scriptures were halted in all public educational institutions within their jurisdiction.[98]

Wisconsin Catholics rejoiced at the decision, but Protestant reaction was equally swift and, for the most part, unsympathetic. A committee of the Methodist Episcopal conference meeting in New York repudiated the ruling as "Un-American and pagan," and the Reverend J. R. Creighton of the Summerfield Methodist Church in Wisconsin went so far even to imply that the Supreme Court had been influenced in its decision by the demands of the "Romish hierarchy."

These sentiments were also echoed by the New York Presbyterian General Assembly, while in Wisconsin the Winnebago Presbytery added its own declaration that daily Scriptural readings in public institutions were essential "to the full, complete, and healthy moral and educational development of the youth of our state and country." Thereafter, it became the object of all these religious

---

98 *Madison Daily Democrat*, February 1, 1890, p. 4; Feb. 2, p. 4; June 18, p. 1. *Milwaukee Journal*. March 18, 1890, p. 1. *Milwaukee Sentinel*, March 19, 1890, p. 1. See also Bascom, p. 60.

groups to reverse the high court's decision and restore the Bible to its former place in the public school curriculum.[99]

In fact, so disturbing was the thought of outlawing Bible-reading that many, like the "Patriot" writing in the *Madison Daily Democrat*, saw in both the recent Supreme Court ruling and the Bennett Law agitation, one general scheme for the eventual destruction of the public school system. "You perceive the plan!" he warned. "First oust the Bible from our public schools, then claim school money on the ground that, according to the dictates of conscience, they cannot send their children to such a school...."[100]

To further substantiate this fear, attention was drawn to the fact that in New Jersey, Bishop Winand M. Wigger of the Newark diocese, had threatened excommunication of Catholic parents who sent their children to public schools, while a statement from a Louisville Catholic organ, reprinted in Milwaukee's own *Columbia* newspaper, had labeled the state school system "Spartan, despotic, heathenish, anti-Christian, [and] anti-Catholic."[101] Furthermore, articles appearing in the *American Catholic Quarterly Review* and other church magazines had for a long time attacked both the moral climate of such institutions and the assumption that Catholics should be made to support two school systems.

The Reverend Francis Chatard, for example, asserted that Catholics should either receive their fair share of the school fund or be exempt from taxation for the support of public education, while another made reference to the state's "pauper school system"

---

99 *Milwaukee Sentinel*, April 8, 1890, p. 9; April 14, p. 4; April 21, p. 3. *Milwaukee Journal*, April 11, 1890, p. 1. *Madison Daily Democrat*, April 11, 1890, p. 3; April 13, p. 3; May 27, p. 1.
100 *Madison Daily Democrat*, February 2, 1890, p. 4.
101 *Bennett Law Clippings*, I, 15, 35, 68; *Milwaukee Sentinel*, February 7, 1890, p. 4.

whose "Godless schools" should be made to depend on other than Catholic funds.[102] The *Menomonie NordStern* was even more specific, however, when it reportedly stated: "If we are strong enough to destroy the Republican party . . . and to give all the offices to the Democrats, they will promise us, not only all the school-houses, but all the school fund, too. . . ."[103]

In short, at a time when traditional religious antagonists were uniting in their opposition to the Bennett Law, such suspicion threatened to disrupt the newly developed harmony. Some Lutherans were suspicious of the ultimate outcome of a victory by the Democrats and predicted that triumph in the upcoming election simply meant the propagation of the Catholic faith throughout the state.[104] The *Lutheran Observer*, published in Philadelphia by the Evangelical Lutheran Church of Pennsylvania, called the unprecedented religious alliance "a strange and humiliating spectacle."[105]

The Bible-reading case, as it turned out, was not capable of permanently damaging union of the anti-Bennett Law forces, but it did serve to underline the basic division between Catholics and Lutherans, which only an extraordinarily strong issue could ever have bridged.

---

102 Francis S. Chatard, "Are Catholics Right?" in *American Catholic Quarterly Review*, XV (1890), 566-575. Thomas Becker, "Secular Education," in *American Catholic Quarterly Review*, XVII (1892), 176-190. See also Brother Azarias, "Religion in Education," in *American Catholic Quarterly Review*, XVI (1891), 760-778; Brother Barbas, "Professor Fisher on 'Unsectarianism' in the Common Schools," in *American Catholic Quarterly Review*, XIV (1889), 505-515; and Michael Hennessy, "Why Education Should be Free," in *American Catholic Quarterly Review*, XVI (1891), 806-817.
103 *Bennett Law Clippings*, I, 11.
104 *Milwaukee Sentinel*, June 10, 1890, p. 3; June 15, p. 1.
105 *The Lutheran Observer*, August 29, 1890, reprinted in the *Wisconsin State Journal*, September 13, 1890, p. 2.

V

The Bennett Law Controversy in Politics

As a result of these open attacks upon the Bennett Law by the two strongest religious groups in the State of Wisconsin, the Democrats at last felt compelled to bring the issue into the political arena. The first Democrat to do so was John Hinsey, who on March 20, 1890, declared unequivocally that the Bennett measure was a "foolish piece of legislation" and ought to be repealed. Like most members of his party, however, he also stated that he was in favor of compelling parents whose children attended parochial schools to send them in addition to schools where English was taught. But for this purpose he believed the compulsory education law already on the books would have sufficed.[106]

It was this flat demand for repeal, coupled with the contradictory endorsement of the very thing that the measure was designed to promote, that proved so exasperating to Governor Hoard, who stubbornly insisted on the principle of the law and saw such ambivalent statements as mere pandering to the selfish desires of a group of foreign-born voters who placed their own national

---

106 *Milwaukee Sentinel*, March 20, 1890, p. 1.

pride above the welfare of the state and even of their own children. Other Republicans, however, were more inclined to believe that by compromising on at least some of the less important issues, both principle and party could be saved from disastrous defeat at the polls.

The first real test that the new law faced occurred in the Milwaukee city election held in the spring of 1890. Religious groups in the metropolis had for a long time been serving notice through resolutions, circular letters to possible candidates, and their newly formed anti-Bennett Law clubs, that they would be an active force in the upcoming campaign. The Republicans confronted the issue first in their convention on March 22, 1890. At that time, Henry C. Payne, a moderate Republican who did not believe in supporting a losing issue, was nominated to become chairman of the Republican State Central Committee and of the city convention. In speaking before the assembled body, Payne drew attention to the fact that the continued agitation of the Bennett Law question threatened to undermine party unity and consequently Republican political control in the state. Their main purpose, therefore, must be to allay any fear on the part of the public that their party was indifferent to the rights of conscience or of the right of the parent to choose the school in which his child would be educated.

At the same time, however, Republicans could not disclaim their belief that a knowledge of English was necessary for all American children and that compulsory education for all up to a certain age was a necessary provision to prevent child labor. With this in mind, Payne recommended a platform stating that the Bennett Law should either be amended or a new law enacted that would prove less objectionable to the various religious and nationality groups while attaining similar ends. The convention, after agreeing to this platform statement, renominated incumbent mayor Thomas H. Brown as its standard-bearer in the upcoming municipal election.[107]

Nevertheless, Payne's conciliatory message did not prove to be as acceptable to all elements as he had hoped. A number of influential Republicans, as well as most Democrats, denounced the platform as a clear case of political fence-straddling. Editor Horace Rublee of the *Milwaukee Sentinel* called the speech a "blunder" and declared that only a position of strong support for the Bennett Law could result in victory for the party.[108] German Lutheran groups, too, were unhappy with Payne's recommendations, but for a different reason. At a meeting of 200 delegates from various Milwaukee churches, they resolved that the Republican declaration of principles was unacceptable and endorsed only those candidates who pledged themselves to absolute repeal of the measure.[109] In the next month, these and other resolutions were also endorsed by German Lutheran synod conferences in Indiana and Michigan.[110]

The Democratic convention met on March 24, 1890 and quickly made known its own view that the law was "uselessly harsh and unjust" and therefore should be repealed in the next legislative session. Republicans were chided for slandering the good name of the state in their references to the supposed number of children who were not attending school, and they were also accused of unjustly impugning the motives of religious opponents of the law.

---

107 The various city papers of Milwaukee at this time were naturally full of news concerning both party conventions and the short campaign that followed. See, for example, *Milwaukee Journal*, March 22, 1890, p. 1.
108 *Madison Daily Democrat*, March 25, 1890, p. 1.
109 *Milwaukee Journal*, March 24, 1890, p. 4.
110 *Milwaukee Journal*, April 11, 1890, p. 1; April 12, p. 1; June 9, p. 1.

To lead the Democratic Party in the upcoming elections, George W. Peck, a humorist and mildly renowned author of the book *Peck's Bad Boy*, was nominated for mayor.[111]

In his acceptance speech, Peck once more reiterated the Democratic position that the law was uncalled for. "Let our public schools stand," he said, "and let those who pay for private schools without asking anybody's assistance teach their children their own religion, and may God bless them all as long as they live."[112] In a speech to the South Side Turners' organization a few days later, moreover, he touched upon another fear of the Germans when he alleged that the Bennett Law was merely the first step toward prohibition of the sale and manufacture of alcoholic beverages.

In truth, members of the state's Prohibition Party did favor a compulsory education law, but their platform never specifically endorsed the Bennett enactment, and there is no evidence to support the belief that any state official saw prohibition as the ultimate goal of that law. In any event, the *Milwaukee Sentinel* denounced Peck's comment as "rot,"[113] and John Nagle, editor of the *Manitowoc Pilot* noted in a scathing review of the speech that the candidate had even gone so far as to mention that he himself liked an occasional glass of beer. "How that affects the Bennett law," the editor gibed, "no one can really see."[114]

A number of Democrats were also disturbed by their Party's platform statements. In fact, several hundred signed a protest making known their belief that the Bennett Law was both useful and necessary and should not have become a municipal issue.[115]

---

111 See, e.g., *Milwaukee Journal*, March 24-25, 1890, p. 1.
112 *Milwaukee Journal*, March 25, 1890, p. 4.
113 *Milwaukee Sentinel*, March 30, 1890, p. 4.
114 *Milwaukee Sentinel*, April 5, 1890, p. 4.
115 *Milwaukee Sentinel*, March 30, 1890, p. 1.

Even the *Madison Daily Democrat* criticized the platform, along with the Republicans, for being "cowardly" in their willingness to abandon the public school system for a few petty political offices.[116] And finally from Illinois, where a similar controversy had erupted over the Edwards Bill, the normally Democratic *Chicago Herald* editorialized (though with a somewhat disconcerting display of nativism): "If this country is to be fit to live in fifty years from now, the hordes of foreigners who take refuge in it every year must be Americanized. They must be educated and must be compelled to learn the English language."[117]

Despite such disapproving statements, however, the opponents of the Bennett Law were victorious. After a short but energetic campaign in which nearly every Lutheran and Catholic voter was visited by his clergyman with the goal of enlisting his support, on April 2, 1890, George W. Peck was elected Mayor of Milwaukee over the Republican incumbent by a margin of 6,965 votes.[118]

The *Herold*, the *Columbia*, the *Germania*, and other German Catholic and Lutheran papers rejoiced at this "wonderful victory for Germandom over narrow-hearted nativism," and the *Seebote* declared: "We will not be robbed of the dear speech in which our mothers taught us our first songs. The German language shall be maintained in America." Across the country, other sympathetic newspapers that had been eagerly awaiting the outcome of this first political contest involving the Bennett Law, also commented,

---
116 *Madison Daily Democrat*, March 28, 1890, p. 2.
117 Reprinted in *Madison Daily Democrat*, March 27, 1890, p. 2.
118 See, for example, *Milwaukee Journal*, April 2, 1890, p. 1. As Bayrd Still points out in his history of Milwaukee (p. 297), "the participation of about 80 percent of the registered voters was in part made possible by the coincidence of the funeral of Archbishop Heiss and election day, a situation which permitted Catholic workers to take time off for the funeral and at the same time support the church at the polls."

declaring that the election victory had been a blow against all such "Puritanical interference" by the state in strictly private institutions.[119]

Nevertheless, contrary opinions indicated that the Republicans were not yet ready to give up the contest. An anonymous letter printed in the *River Falls Journal* called upon all those who loved liberty to break through "the ominous clouds of priestly intolerance" that "menace our republican institutions,"[120] and encouraging editorial comment from papers in New York, Pittsburgh, Duluth, Minneapolis-St. Paul, Detroit, Baltimore, Philadelphia, and other cities throughout the country made clear that the Bennett Law had become much more than a local issue.

At this time also, an "American Catholic" wrote to the editor of the *Chicago Tribune* that ecclesiastical politics were responsible for the controversy surrounding the Bennett Law in Wisconsin. It was the "old-country priests," he said, who sought to maintain their control over immigrant Catholics, and it was also this clique, fearing for their stronghold in Milwaukee, who had used the anti-Bennett Law agitation in the recent election to strengthen their own position.[121] The *Chicago Times*, chief Democratic paper in the Middle West, declared: "If the state follows Milwaukee, the Democrats will meet a deserved defeat. The State of Wisconsin has the right to Americanize its foreign population."[122]

---

119 A good source of general press comment on the Milwaukee municipal election in papers printed in Wisconsin and throughout the United States is the article "Compulsory English Education: The Bennett Law in Wisconsin," published in *Public Opinion*, IX (April 12, 1890), 1-4. See also *Madison Daily Democrat*, April 4, 1890, p. 1; *Milwaukee Sentinel*, April 15, 1890, p. 4; and Kellogg, "The Bennett Law," pp. 21-22.
120 *River Falls Journal*, April 3, 1890, in *Bennett Law Clippings*, I.
121 *Chicago Tribune*, April 10, 1890, p. 7.
122 *Chicago Times*, April 3, 1890, quoted in Kellogg, "The Bennett Law," p. 22.

On April 2, the same day as the Milwaukee election, Governor Hoard made a widely publicized address before the Waukesha Teachers' Convention in which he further outlined his position on the controversial law. In this address, the governor expressed shock and dismay that any individual, church, or newspaper in the land could be found to oppose the acquisition of only "a small amount of American education," especially when the inability to speak English was so clearly a disadvantage in this country. Moreover, he asserted, the state certainly had the right to provide for the secular education of its inhabitants, and if certain parents neglected their duty, it was only proper that they be compelled by law to fulfill it. No interference with religion was implied so long as the state's educational requirements were satisfied.

But then, he went on, why this outcry against what was an eminently necessary enactment? At first he had believed the opposition stemmed from misunderstanding or ignorance of what the law intended, but now he saw behind it the evidence of design, a selfish concern by some for their own "bread and butter" rather than the future welfare of their children. Thus, pointing once again to the large numbers of young people who did not attend school, he remarked:

> There they stand, an army of ignorance growing up in our midst, denied by cupidity and bigotry combined, the privileges of even the free schools of our state. A large proportion are purposely kept in this condition. And yet, my countrymen, the air is full of the pleadings of priests and politicians, that this blessed condition of things may continue, that this illiteracy so conducive to certain ideas of what constitutes religion and morals may not be disturbed by the force of law.[123]

---

123 *Milwaukee Journal*, April 2, 1890, p. 1; *Milwaukee Sentinel*, April 3, 1890,

In all this, he further believed, the future of the common school system was at stake, for if the state could not require a certain caliber of secular education in all institutions, then it had no right even to compel attendance. Thus, what should have been only a question of necessary instruction, had now become a true contest between church and state, and he advised that all those who believed in "rendering unto Caesar the things that are Caesar's and unto God the things that are God's" must support the side of the state. Moreover, he felt that the result of the controversy in the end could not but harm the churches themselves, as young people realized the folly of the stand taken by their clergymen.

To a group of Lutheran ministers who visited him in his office in an effort to convince him to modify his position on the law, Governor Hoard remarked that "by taking your church into the political arena and there making of it a football to be kicked about by contending politicians, you will live to rue the day." Indeed, if they persisted in using their religious authority to block human progress, he told them, "you will eventually lose your position of leadership and the respect of the young men and young women now in your church for your selfish action." Already he reported having received letters from such disillusioned youngsters who stated that if their church could not prosper without keeping children in ignorance of the English language, then they could no longer remain a part of it.[124]

---

p. 4. See also Kellogg, "Interview Notes," p. 5.
124 Quoted in Rankin, pp. 132-133. See also *Milwaukee Sentinel*, April 6, 1890, p. 11, for an interview with the governor and his comments on the matter. William D. Hoard, "Account of an Incident in which a group of Lutheran ministers visited Hoard in his office to speak out against the Bennett Law (summer of 1890)" was written from memory by the former governor and presented to Dr. Kellogg in an interview at his home in August, 1918. Copy preserved in Kellogg Papers.

But neither side proved willing to give in to the other, and as the spring days quickly gave way to summer, it became clear that in the November election the Bennett Law, so inconspicuous in its beginnings, would become the main issue for all parties. Both the Catholics and the Lutherans were determined to see that the hated measure was repealed. Thus, from May 26 to 28, the Catholic Benevolent Societies of Milwaukee met in convention, attended by such prominent church leaders as the Bishops Katzer and Flasch and Monsignor Augustine Zeininger. Once more speakers reiterated the now-common charge that the law had been the work of "nativists and advocates of paternalism." Encouraged by the results of the Milwaukee mayoral election, delegates to these conventions also pledged to support only those candidates for state office who would vow to repeal the law, if elected.[125]

A new factor was introduced at this meeting, however, in a speech given by Bishop Frederick Katzer of Green Bay. Katzer, who was later appointed Archbishop of Milwaukee, succeeding Michael Heiss who died in March, had already become the leader of the Catholic anti-Bennett Law forces in Wisconsin. Although John Ireland, who opposed his nomination for the high church office, wrote to Cardinal Gibbons that the Bishop of the Green Bay diocese was "'a man thoroughly German and thoroughly unfit to be an archbishop,'" he nevertheless enjoyed the continuing support of many fellow German-American Catholics in the state who were determined to safeguard both their religious and national heritage.[126]

---

125 *Milwaukee Journal*, May 27, 1890, p. 1; *Milwaukee Sentinel*, May 28, 1890, p. 1; *Madison Daily Democrat*, May 28, 1890, p. 1.

126 Katzer, a native of Austria, was named Archbishop of Milwaukee by the Vatican in December, 1890, against the wishes of many English-speaking Catholic clergymen, including Archbishop Ireland of St. Paul and Cardinal Gibbons

Speaking before the Milwaukee convention, Katzer declared that the Bennett Law was merely the first step toward eventual total suppression of religion by the state. Furthermore, its passage had been engineered by the Freemasons, who—the Bishop charged—were even then at work throughout the state and nation in an effort to undermine Christianity. Indeed, he claimed to have positive proof of this in testimony of a former Mason that such a law as the one now in effect had been sought five years before by the Grand Lodge of Wisconsin.[127]

Although this charge was repeated and officially sanctioned in an article by the Reverend Francis Chatard published in the *American Catholic Quarterly Review*, members of the Masonic Order quickly and indignantly denied the claim. J.W. Laflin, Grand Secretary of the Order in Wisconsin, expressed surprise that the Bishop could be so woefully ignorant of the basic principles of Masonry, while a less temperate spokesman for the organization called the Catholic clergyman "a willful, unscrupulous, unmitigated liar."[128] Governor

---

of Baltimore. These priests would have preferred someone who was less sympathetic to the complaints of German immigrants who sought to preserve their language and customs in national parishes within the Church. A conservative, the new archbishop also strongly opposed Ireland's Faribault-Stillwater plan for a compromise settlement of the school question and sought papal condemnation of Catholic membership in *all* secret societies, not just the Masons. See Blied, pp. 46-81 and Ellis, *Gibbons*, pp. 364-373. His outspoken comments on many of these issues, in fact, were represented at the time as evidence that he was not the best choice for this high church office. The *Milwaukee Sentinel* commented: "His appointment may be acceptable to the more radical German element in the church, but it will not be at all pleasing to most of the Irish clergy." December 23, 1890, p. 1.

127 *Milwaukee Sentinel*, May 28, 1890, p. 1. In his address the Bishop said flatly: "The law is nothing but a blow aimed at the church, coming from the Free Masons."

128 *Milwaukee Sentinel*, May 29, 1890, p. 4. A notice from Green Bay, June 4, 1890, stated that Bishop Katzer was planning to sue Charles W. Felker for having called him a "liar." No further mention of this suit is made after this date, however. See *Bennett Law Clippings*, I.

Hoard, in a confidential letter to Senator John C. Spooner in Washington, expressed the belief that the attack against the Masons had only done injury to the anti-Bennett Law cause and ended with the pious observation: "All things work together for good to those who love the Lord."[129]

Nevertheless, the Lutheran groups were also preparing to martial their forces for the upcoming gubernatorial election. On June 4, 1890, the anti-Bennett Law convention, proposed in May, was called to order in Milwaukee. Christian Koerner, legal editor of the *Germania* and the leading opponent of the Bennett Law in Wisconsin, was named chairman of the meeting. In his opening remarks, he said that the issue was one involving both Know-Nothingism and ignorance and emerged from a "stupid and bungling hatred against the foreign-born citizen."[130] Yet the enemy had been defeated in the spring municipal elections, and it was possible that with hard work they could be beaten once again.

First, however, the Lutherans had drawn up and endorsed a substitute bill, very much like the Bennett Law with the single omission of an English language clause. Surprisingly, this bill, written by editor Koerner, also contained a provision for securing various statistics from denominational schools, a proposal that only a year before had elicited outspoken criticism of the Pond bill.

Should this substitute measure be rejected, however, as indeed it subsequently was, the Lutherans were determined to fight.[131]

---

129 Letter to John C. Spooner, dated May 31, 1890, in Hoard, *Private Letter Books*, 17:15.
130 *Milwaukee Journal*, June 4, 1890, pp. 1-4. *Milwaukee Sentinel*, June 5, 1890, p. 1.
131 The Lutheran substitute bill was reprinted in *Madison Daily Democrat*, June 1, 1890, p. 1.

Under the supervision of a central executive committee with headquarters in Milwaukee, the state was divided into districts so that every city, village, and township could arrange meetings and speeches for the fall campaign.[132] The platform adopted by the delegates declared:

> As patriotic citizens, maintaining human rights both civil and religious, advocating sound principles of education, and with no enmity toward the English language, opposed, however, to all measures tending to oppress the immigrated citizens, or to suppress their native tongue, we call upon all those who cherish liberty, regardless of party and nationality, to join us in the effort to have this unnecessary, unjust, and discord-breeding measure repealed.[133]

The importance attached to maintaining the German cultural tradition and language also became vividly clear in the speeches that were given at the convention. Conrad Krez, for example, denied that German was a foreign language and stated that anyone who would support a law aimed at its suppression could easily commit high treason. "No," he vowed, "we will not allow our language to be trodden down and taken from us."[134]

August Ross, a manager of the *Germania*, revealed a similar concern when he observed that there seemed to exist in the United States a peculiar "naturalizing or Americanizing rage." He suggested sarcastically that victims of this "mania" post signs in all harbors along the eastern seaboard inscribed with the words, "English is spoken here." In a more serious vein, however, he warned that

---

132 Otto F. Hattstaedt, *History of the Southern Wisconsin District of the Lutheran Synod of Missouri, Ohio, and Other States* (St. Louis, 1928), trans. Wis. Hist. Soc. *Records Survey*, W.P.A. (Madison, 1941), p. 77.
133 *Milwaukee Journal*, June 4, 1890, p. 1.
134 *Milwaukee Sentinel*, June 5, 1890, p. 1.

the Bennett Law could only be viewed as the legal expression of a desire to force all immigrants to abandon their mother tongue and use English exclusively. Moreover, he would remind Germans that effective temperance laws depended on fully Americanized citizens. Once all the schools are under state control, Ross hinted darkly, "there is room for hope that all children will be impressed with the belief that all beverages except water are of evil, and then the way is paved for a crusade against brewers, whose property must be seized, and those who prefer beer and wine will either die soon or emigrate and leave to us the field for the formation of an English-American temperance nation, and then the millennium will have come. . . ."[135]

Despite such obviously panicky statements, however, the meeting also produced some remarkably cogent arguments from those delegates whose opposition to the law was tempered by an understanding of the factors responsible for the major share of apprehension and strife. Among these individuals was Professor Rasmus B. Anderson, who revealed some of this unbiased attitude when he objected to being introduced to the convention as a Norwegian rather than as an American. Originally a Republican Party member, he had supported the law on condition that certain objectionable features would soon be modified. But the refusal of the governor to accept the suggested changes had eventually driven him to the side of the opposition. Nevertheless, he was proud of the fact that he had often defended the public schools to his fellow Norwegians and had stated publicly that if the Lutheran Church could not exist alongside of the public school, then it might perish and he would say "peace be with its ashes." Moreover, on the upper right hand corner of all his letter

---
135 *Milwaukee Journal*, June 4, 1890, p. 4.

paper he had printed the words: "Opposition to the American common school is treason to our country."[136]

Nevertheless, although he had little fear that the law was aimed at total extinction of any foreign tongue, he declared that the law was entirely unnecessary because the English language required no protection. It was already sweeping through the country like some "all-powerful giant" and would soon be spoken universally anyway. The Bennett Law merely served to provoke "nationality indignation among the foreign groups and fanaticism in certain religious sects." Moreover, it had been written in a careless manner and was full of blunders, such as the district clause and the provision for requiring consecutive attendance at school.

Professor Anderson then gave a summary of the problems involved in the law, which revealed as acute a perception of the reasons behind the controversy as any given during the debate. He said:

> When foreigners have crossed the Atlantic, they come to a stream. There are two ways of crossing it—either by swimming or bridging it. The fanatics on the side of the Bennett law would force all to the harsh and hasty method of swimming; that is, they would have them cast off their clothing (i.e., their customs, language, etc.) and emerge on the other shore naked. The opponents of the law would bridge the stream and enable the foreigners to pass over, thus preserving to them all their knowledge of European literature, history, and customs.
>
> The complaint of all foreigners is that their children learn English too readily here; that they soon are unable to converse with their parents in their native tongue. The English language cannot be repressed; it is bound to

---

136   Anderson, *Life Story*, pp. 597-598.

prevail in America. The problem which the Bennett law seeks to solve will work itself out in due time. The second generation of foreigners never fails to know the English language. To compulsorily Americanize foreigners coming to this country is disadvantageous to us Americans.[137]

The validity of Anderson's observations could be readily discerned from the comments of those who sent letters of support to the anti-Bennett Law convention. Over and over again appeared the stated belief that enmity toward foreign languages was at the root of the new law, and throughout there was expressed the determination to see that it was finally repealed.[138] In the weeks that followed the convention, numerous churches throughout Wisconsin, a conference of Lutheran teachers, and the various synodal groups of the state ratified the platform adopted at Milwaukee.[139] Thus, the Catholics and the Lutherans now appeared to be solidly united in their political goals concerning the statute.

Nevertheless, a speech given by Archbishop Ireland of the St. Paul diocese on June 10, 1890, before the annual convention of the National Education Association, revealed the very real division that still existed between the German- and English-speaking elements of the Catholic Church. Archbishop Ireland had, of course, been one of the two bishops at Rome in 1886, who had begun the opposition against Father Peter Abbelen's petition for national parishes. Since then, he had become a leading representative of the anti-Cahensly forces within the church, stressing at every opportunity the belief that all immigrants should strive to become American in outlook. Thus, he wrote:

---

137 *Milwaukee Sentinel*, June 5, 1890, p. 1.
138 Quoted in *Milwaukee Journal*, June 4, 1890, p. 2.
139 *Milwaukee Journal*, July 3, 1890, p. 1; July 24, p. 6.

> The spirit of our institutions should, of course, be made to pervade our foreign-born populations. . . . No encouragement must be given to social and political organizations or methods which perpetuate in this country foreign ideas and customs. An Irish-American, a German-American, or a French-American is an intolerable anomaly. We receive from America the right to vote as Americans, for America's weal, and if we cannot use our privileges as Americans, we should surrender them. Efforts to concentrate immigrants in social groups and to retard their Americanization should be steadily frowned down. There are in America self-constituted leaders of foreign-born citizens who speak of Americanization as a term of reproach; with these men public opinion should deal severely.[140]

Now, before the Education Association, Archbishop Ireland expressed an opinion on compulsory education that alarmed many Catholics and aroused the ire of Wisconsin's anti-Bennett Law forces. In his speech, he told the assembled delegates that he was "unreservedly in favor" of state compulsory education laws, even though he recognized the original and prior right of the parent to educate his child in a way suitable to himself and his religion. Such measures were necessary for the safety of the Republic, he declared, since generally the uneducated man could not vote intelligently. Yet, at the same time, their application was contingent upon the inability or refusal of the parent to see to it that his child was properly educated.

Those laws recently enacted in several Midwestern states did not violate this requirement, he believed, and their only objectionable features were to be found in a few specific clauses that could undoubtedly be amended. At the same time, however,

---

140 John Ireland, *The Church and Modern Society* (Chicago and New York, 1896), pp. 188-189.

Ireland was disturbed by the completely secular nature of these public schools. He reminded his audience that in their mutual fear that Protestants or Catholics might gain some advantage over the other, the school was delivered into the hands of unbelievers and secularists.

To prevent the situation in which the mass of American children would grow up without religion, he suggested that the regular state school be permeated with the religion of the majority of the children of the land, be it "as Protestant as Protestantism can be." It was understood, of course, that Catholic children might also have the privilege of continued attendance at their own schools. This arrangement could be accomplished by following the English scheme whereby secular instruction given in denominational schools was paid for by the state according to the ability of each pupil to pass an examination before state officials. Another possible solution was the "Poughkeepsie Plan" in which the school board rented the parish schools for the regular school day, and religious instruction was given after hours.[141]

For these remarks, Ireland was severely censured by Bishop Katzer of Green Bay, Father Abbelen of Milwaukee, and other members of the Catholic Church in Wisconsin. Some German Catholic papers even suggested that Ireland had lost the faith and was promoting Protestantism, while others discovered disloyalty to the Church in his refusal to denounce the immorality of the public school system.[142] Eventually the address was reported adversely to the Holy See, and the rumor quickly spread that Ireland had been

---

141 Ireland, pp. 199-214. See also a very clear explanation of this speech and its meaning, written by Archbishop Ireland to Cardinal Gibbons after the latter had been asked by Pope Leo XIII, himself, to comment on its content and validity—in Ellis, *Documents,* pp. 469-475.
142 Ellis, *Documents,* pp. 471, 472, 475.

summoned to Rome to explain his position before the Pope. The Archbishop denied this, however, as well as the charge that the Catholic Church was opposed to compulsory education.

Nevertheless, James Cardinal Gibbons was asked his opinion of Ireland's speech by Pope Leo XIII. The former, having received a detailed letter of explanation from Ireland, vigorously defended his fellow clergyman with regard to his ideas on education, as well as his religious loyalty. In the end, the Pope did not see fit to censure the Archbishop of St. Paul for his statements, but this dispute was but one further manifestation of the controversy between Irish and German Catholics so near the surface and ready to burst forth at any provocation in the last decade of the 19th century.[143]

The foregoing events made it impossible to avoid the Bennett Law issue in the November election. Likewise, for the Republicans the choice of a candidate was all but eliminated, for the party could not be placed in the position of repudiating Governor Hoard. Nevertheless, the veteran party leaders did not share the Governor's idealistic attitude toward the law nor his confidence in ultimate victory on this issue. Henry Payne, Chairman of the State Central Committee, had already attempted some conciliation toward the opposition in his speech before the Milwaukee mayoralty election. In addition, a pre-convention meeting of Republicans in May revealed a deep-seated anxiety concerning the outcome of the future statewide elections, and

---

143   Ellis, *Documents*, pp. 469-475; *Milwaukee Daily Journal*, October 31, 1890, p. 1 (Ireland's denial of rumors regarding a summons to Rome). Governor Hoard said of Ireland's speech before the National Teachers' Association: "I consider the good bishop has helped the educational cause grandly even though we may not agree with all his recommendations. He is a noble patriotic man and such men cannot go far wrong." See Hoard, *Private Letter Books*, 17:197.

in June a private meeting between Senator Spooner and Payne, to which a delegation of Wisconsin Lutherans was admitted and in which the future platform was discussed, pointedly excluded the governor.[144]

Similar concern about the forthcoming election was evident in the private correspondence between such eminent Republicans as Congressman Ellis P. Haugen and the former governor, now U.S. Secretary of Agriculture, Jeremiah M. Rusk. The latter in particular expressed the professional politician's concern for party harmony and ultimate control of state offices. Thus, in October and November 1889, he was already writing to his friend Colonel Henry Casson that it might be necessary to repudiate the Bennett Law in the next state platform, even if the governor's personal feelings were hurt, since it was not safe to make a fight that would cripple their German Republican support. He himself would take the first opportunity to make a public statement denouncing the law in order to "put myself right with my German friends as heretofore."

Then, as a Republican defeat was registered in the spring election in Milwaukee, Rusk's letters became filled with nervous calculations and inquiries as to the number of German Lutheran and German Catholic votes within the various districts of the state. Another of his fears was that the Prohibition Party might join with

---

144 *Madison Daily Democrat*, May 1, 1890, p. 1; June 25, p. 1. Neither Payne nor Spooner had supported Hoard for the gubernatorial nomination in 1888, and his conduct with regard to the Bennett Law had done little to change their opinion with regard to his political acumen. Spooner believed Hoard's championship of the law to be a "'barefaced and asinine' blunder." Payne also tried unsuccessfully to convince the Wisconsin Congressional delegation that pressure ought to be brought to bear against the governor to persuade him not to run for re-election. Dorothy Canfield Fowler, *John Coit Spooner, Defender of Presidents* (New York, 1961), p. 146.

the Republicans and thus destroy forever any hope of German support. The situation appeared critical, for as Rusk wrote to his friend, "unless some understanding is had, you and I will never live long enough to again see the Republican Party in power after the next election."

He would not therefore actually work against the re-nomination of Hoard for governor, but he felt that the ticket should include as many Norwegians and German Lutheran candidates as possible to woo the foreign vote. Compulsory education was undoubtedly a sound principle, he said, but the law of 1879 would have been sufficient, particularly with an election at stake. Moreover, the rigid attitude of men like Superintendent Thayer or Governor Hoard was "absolutely insane" and could only bring disaster to the Republican Party.[145]

But if Rusk, Payne, Spooner, and others counseled a policy of prudence and compromise, Congressman Ellis P. Haugen saw only defeat and disgrace in such a move. As one of the original supporters of the 1879 compulsory education law, Haugen was naturally a staunch advocate of the new statute and saw no reason to believe that it interfered with civil or religious liberties of the parent. In answer to a questionnaire circulated by the *North*, chief Scandinavian paper of the Northwest, he stated that whether or not the foreign-born citizen attempted to perpetuate the customs and language of his fatherland was a matter of personal choice, but he considered it the duty of an adopted American citizen "to assist the state in its endeavors to familiarize his children with the language of the country whose

---

145 Jeremiah M. Rusk, *Letters of Jeremiah M. Rusk to Colonel Henry Casson* [in Rusk Papers, MSS in possession of the Wis. Hist. Soc.], 3 (July 23, 1889—December 6, 1889), 304-305, 422-423; 4 (December 6, 1889—May 21, 1890), 464-465, 465-466, 478-479.

laws they must obey, and in whose government they will have a voice."[146]

Accordingly, Congressman Haugen cautioned against apologizing for the Bennett Law, straddling the issue, or in any way showing signs of irresolution and fear. The Party might lose votes in the eastern half of the state and a few "extremists" might even bolt the convention, but since this was not strictly a partisan issue, the Democrats would have a similar problem. In addition, the alliance between Lutherans, who objected to details of the law, and Catholics, who opposed it in principle, was unlikely to last. Consequently, he was angry that Payne, Spooner, and the others appeared so demoralized by the Milwaukee election, and he insisted that they could still win the final contest if they did not become frightened and abandon the essential principle of the law for a "weak-kneed, vote-catching policy."[147]

Nevertheless, evidence of a serious division in Republican ranks with regard to the Bennett Law continued to emerge as the time for active campaigning approached. Secretary of State Ernst Timme, a popular and influential party member, wrote an article for an eastern magazine entitled, "Why a German Boy Should Become a Good American Citizen." In it, he spoke glowingly of the many fine character traits of German-Americans and rebuked the governor for allegedly implying that they were not always patriotic citizens.[148] Similarly, Senator Spooner was quoted as saying publicly that he would never "'permit any ignorant school board to dictate to me where my little

---

146 Letter to the editor of the *North*, dated April 26, 1890, in Nils P. Haugen, *Letter Books* [Haugen Papers, MSS in possession of the Wis. Hist. Soc.], I (Sept. 19, 1888—May 7, 1890), 452-454.
147 Haugen, *Letter Books*, I: 275-277, 369-370, 387-388 402-403, 447, 460-461; II: 14, 41-42, 85, 104-109, 181-183, 301, 341.
148 *Milwaukee Journal*, July 24, 1890, p. 1.

boy shall go to school.'" Congressman Haugen pointed out that such statements could only damage party chances for victory since compromise on non-essential provisions was unlikely to convince many anti-Bennett Law people to vote for Hoard, while it would very likely drive away the law's most earnest supporters.[149]

Meanwhile, other signs of unrest also appeared. Eleventh ward Republicans in Milwaukee forcibly ejected a Bennett Law advocate and passed resolutions in favor of repeal,[150] while in New York the influential, nationally important Union League deplored such legislation for its interference with parental rights.[151] Perhaps the attitude of many apprehensive Republican politicians was best summed up in a remark overheard at the spring convention in Milwaukee. Having reviewed the work of his fellow delegates, one said frankly: "It's a d—d good platform, but I do not want to sink upon it."[152]

At the convention on August 27-28, however, Governor Hoard continued to stress the principle involved in the measure. He was clearly puzzled and exasperated by the refusal of many party members, particularly those in Washington, to support his stand on the Bennett Law, and a barrage of confidential letters was fired off explaining his position anew and asking why they did not make their own statements as forceful. In one reply to criticism from Congressman Myron McCord, he charged that he and his colleagues must be getting their understanding of the controversy from some "unreal" source.

The governor was not opposed to amending the law if any part interfered with the rights of an individual, church or school, but

---
149 Quoted in Haugen, *Letter Books*, II, 85.
150 *Milwaukee Sentinel*, March 20, 1890, p. 1.
151 *Milwaukee Journal*, October 4, 1890, p. 2.
152 Quoted in *Milwaukee Journal*, May 1, 1890, p. 2.

his own speaking tours throughout the state had convinced him that, in the main, the people were behind him in his defense of the public school system. They were not, in short, "time serving politicians ready to cry 'Good Lord or good Devil' as may best suit the occasion." And yet what had they heard from the party machine but the demand for compromise and surrender? Governor Hoard was determined not to allow this half-hearted stand to prevail. "I am content to trust the party," he said, "but you will never see me fool enough to mistake for the voice of the party the whispering cry of '*peccavi*' uttered by a lot of cringing politicians who have no more idea of a campaign for principle than of heaven. . . . If we do not stand up like men in the Bennett law issue, the Republican Party will not be able to carry the state on any issue."[153]

To those Republicans at home, he remarked that he did not care if he were re-nominated, but if he were, he wanted to stand on a platform he could respect.[154] This, of course, would include a plank supporting the Bennett Law, for in speech after speech and letter after letter the governor had hammered home the point that the entire future of the public school system was at stake in the matter. If the legislature had no power to pass a compulsory education law, then it had no power to require compulsory taxation for the support of public schools. If the state had no authority with regard to education, then the church had succeeded in capturing secular powers, and ecclesiasticism would soon control the land.

For the governor, this contest was clearly a matter of conviction, far above all party and personal considerations. Indeed, in his championship of state authority, he held almost a religious view of the controversy, as can readily be discerned from the Biblical

---

153 Hoard, *Private Letter Books*, 16:989-996.
154 Quoted in Kellogg, "Interview Notes," p. 4.

phraseology that abounds in his letters to constituents and party leaders. The Democrats, he charged, had "Bent the Knee to Baal," trading the "Lord's Supper for the caucus" in their vote-catching attempts. At times, he said, it made him almost sick of life itself to see these priests, newspapers, and politicians conspiring for their own profit at the expense of the future welfare of the poor children of Wisconsin. At any moment, he expected the very rocks to cry out "For shame, oh! my countrymen, to feed thus on the weak and helpless!" Unless some stand were made now on this issue, he believed, the yoke of ecclesiasticism would soon be about all their necks, and religious fanaticism would have succeeded in throttling the public school system. Therefore, his opponents, particularly the Catholics and the Lutherans, were stiffly reminded that "there is a way which seemeth right unto a man, but the end thereof is death."

On the other hand, the governor expressed confidence to his supporters that the Lord was on their side and their faith in the people would be vindicated. "Do you remember the injunction Moses gave the Israelites?" Hoard asked his chief Democratic supporter, John Nagle. "'Stand still and see the salvation of the Lord.' Do you remember also that other Scriptural phrase, which says, 'He maketh the wrath of man to praise Him.' . . . The present outlook is most encouraging. . . . The heart of the people cannot be corrupted nor intimidated and you are the best apostle in all the Gospel of education. Heaven bless you now and forever. Amen."[155]

---

155   Hoard, *Private Letter Books*, 16:88-90, 112, 229, 231, 289, 345-346; 17:62-63, 101. These are but a few of the literally hundreds of letters in the Hoard collection dealing with the Bennett Law issue. Almost all of them contain some reference to the "principle" involved in upholding the law, and most of them, up to the very day of the election, express the belief that "the people" would one day realize its value and come to support it as the governor did.

For professional politicians concerned about winning votes and holding office, however, such statements were the essence of foolhardiness and a clear vindication of their long held belief that this rank amateur politician who had gained the governorship in his first attempt at elected office was not capable of conducting a winning campaign. Even Congressman Haugen, who favored absolutely no compromise on the matter, was wise enough in the ways of politics to advise the governor not to make rash statements that could be interpreted as attacks upon the Germans as a nationality. Rather, it was safest to hammer away at the Catholics who were lost anyway and impress the Lutherans with the fact that they were merely acting as the tail to the Catholic kite. A reaction might therefore be expected to set in and many Republican votes salvaged from among the ranks of the Lutherans.[156]

As for Rusk, Spooner, and the others, the only thing they considered was the future of the Republican Party in Wisconsin, and if some compromise on this contentious issue were therefore necessary, it could not be helped. To such men, who were aware from reports taken from all districts of the state, that a high percentage of previously Republican voters were switching allegiance to the Democrats, Governor Hoard's optimistic belief that "the people" would support the law was ludicrous—and dangerous. Their dilemma was well understood by a contemporary journalist who remarked that the "hustling Republicans" were faced with the difficult problem of how to re-nominate Hoard without upholding the principles of the Bennett Law.[157]

---

156 Haugen, *Letter Books*, I: 387-388.
157 Duane Mowry, "The Situation in Wisconsin," America, July 24, 1890, in *Bound Bennett Law Pamphlets* (collection in possession of Wis. Hist. Soc.).

Discrete silence in the platform was one possibility, but quite obviously cowardly, while any open statement of support was bound to disgruntle large blocs of voters. The supreme exasperation felt by these Republican Party leaders when confronted with Hoard's statement that he would welcome defeat if it would open the eyes of the people to the danger of ecclesiasticism in politics was expressed clearly by one such leader who said—"There is no doing anything with the d—d fool. He doesn't care whether he wins or is broken."[158]

Nevertheless, it was a foregone conclusion that Hoard would be re-nominated for governor. This was done by acclamation on August 20, 1890, while Michael J. Bennett, who had introduced the bill into the Assembly, was also given the candidacy for second district assemblyman.[159] The platform, however, showed the ambivalence in the minds of many convention delegates. It began by disclaiming any intention of interfering with private and parochial schools, but affirmed both the right and the duty of the state to enact laws necessary for guaranteeing all children sufficient instruction in the legal language of the country. The Bennett Law was called both "wise and humane" in its essential purposes, and its repeal was declared completely unacceptable. However, the convention also recognized the right of the parent or guardian "to select the time of year and the place, whether public

---

158   Hoard, *Private Letter Books*, 17:416-422. In this long letter to a supporter in Chicago, dated September 4, 1890, Governor Hoard once again stressed his belief in the principle of the law and his willingness to go down to defeat while defending it. Thus, as he relates in the letter, he had once declared to a convention delegate that he "would welcome defeat if thereby 'the blood of the martyrs might become the seed of the church.'" But contrary to the statement, quoted in the text, that he did not care if he won or lost, he wrote: "Of course, I did care but I did not propose to be purchased by ambition any more than by money."

159   *Milwaukee Journal*, August 20, 1890, p. 2; *Milwaukee Sentinel*, September 24, 1890, p. 1.

or private and wherever located, in which his child or ward shall receive instruction." Therefore, the delegates pledged themselves willing to modify, or amend, the law to conform to the situation. The Republicans also went on record in support of legislation to prevent child labor and chronic truancy and in opposition to any union between church and state.[160]

In a forceful speech, Governor Hoard accepted this statement of the Republican position with its willingness to amend the law and expressed gratitude for the vote of confidence given him by the convention. "Wisconsin," he said, "stands today with the eyes of the whole nation upon her. From Maine to California comes the inspiring words, 'Stand by the little school house. Forsake not the hope of your children and the progress and perpetuity of the republic.' The Republican Party has always been a party of principle and an exponent of conviction. . . . It now demands for every child that he be given the privileges of his birthright. 'The child that is, the citizen that is to be has appealed to the republican party and all patriotic citizens that he be granted these rights. Shall he appeal in vain?" The answer, the governor fervently believed, could only be found in the willingness of the Republicans to fight for these rights in the upcoming election. Reflecting that conviction, the convention adjourned with the slogan "Stand

---

160 Wisconsin, Secretary of State, *The Blue Book of the State of Wisconsin, 1891* (Milwaukee, 1891), p. 390. In an effort to secure the support of the German press, before the platform was publicly presented in convention, Senator John Spooner had shown a copy of the plank relating to the Bennett Law to the editor of the *Germania*, George Koeppen. At that time, he cautioned the newspaperman not to make any public announcement of approval until after its adoption for fear that Hoard would not support any program satisfactory to the Lutherans. However, in the end, the *Germania* refused to switch its allegiance from the Democratic party, and a later decision to underwrite the friendly *Abendpost*, edited by Paul Bechtner, proved a losing financial enterprise for both Spooner and Payne. See Fowler, pp. 149-150.

by the Little Schoolhouse!" as the official Republican campaign motto.[161]

The Democrats, meanwhile, also met in Milwaukee on August 27, 1890, with a great deal of confidence in the outcome of the November election. Not all Democrats, of course, were in agreement with the anti-Bennett Law position, but those that were had been encouraged by the fact that considerable numbers of formerly Republican Lutherans had begun to join their ranks. In addition, their nominee for governor, George W. Peck, was fresh from his victory in the Milwaukee mayoral contest where his majority had been over 6,000 votes. The nomination speech for Peck given by John Johnston declared that the candidate believed in children acquiring knowledge of the language of the country, but there was no need "of whipping English into children by the legislative lash,"[162] and Peck himself declared that he was ready to repeal the Bennett Law at once if he were elected.[163] In the platform adopted at the convention, the law was declared to be "unnecessary, unwise, unconstitutional, un-American, and undemocratic," as well as a "tyrannical invasion of individual and constitutional rights."[164]

In the aftermath of these two conventions, the divisions between parties and nationalities became even more apparent. The Milwaukee *Seebote* rejoiced in the Democratic platform as a complete victory for "Germanism,"[165] while the *Sentinel* and *Wisconsin State Journal* referred to it variously as a "scurrilous

---

161 Quoted in *Madison Daily Journal*, August 21, 1890, p. 1.
162 Quoted in Alexander McDonald Thomson, *A Political History of Wisconsin* (Milwaukee, 1900), p. 237.
163 *Wisconsin State Journal*, August 28, 1890, p. 1.
164 *Wisconsin Blue Book, 1891*, p. 394.
165 Translated in *Milwaukee Sentinel*, August 29, 1890, p. 4.

manifesto" and as "a conglomeration of demagogy, clap-trap, misrepresentation and unsound and unpatriotic doctrine."[166] German Lutherans and Catholics, on the other hand, were equally quick to denounce the Republican defense of the law.

In addition, there were repercussions among two other political parties in the state—the Prohibition Party and the Union Labor Party. Leaders of the former expressed support for the principles of the Bennett Law, and the state chapter of the Women's Christian Temperance Union (W.C.T.U.) also endorsed the measure. Nevertheless, although local Prohibitionist assemblies in La Crosse, Milwaukee and other cities passed resolutions supporting the Bennett Law, a plank endorsing the measure by name was defeated in the state convention by a vote of 134 to 86. Instead, delegates contented themselves with the simple statement that they favored "a liberal public education in the English language, enforced and supervised by the state."[167]

The Union Labor Party, on the other hand, was unanimously in favor of the compulsory education law and early on vowed that they would support the Republican ticket if it came out squarely for the principles of the measure.[168] In addition, a convention of the Factory Inspectors' Association in New York and a number of important labor leaders championed the Bennett Law as necessary to prevent child labor and raise the level of education among

---

166 *Milwaukee Sentinel*, August 28, 1890, p. 4; *Wisconsin State Journal*, August 28, 1890, p. 2.
167 *Milwaukee Journal*, July 21, 1890, p. 1; *Milwaukee Sentinel*, July 23, 1890, p. 1. Wisconsin W.C.T.U., *Minutes of the Seventeenth Annual Meeting of the Women's Christian Temperance Union of Wisconsin, Held June 3, 4, 5, and 6, 1890, First Methodist Church, Racine, Wis.* (Madison, 1890), p. 23. At this meeting, the W.C.T.U. also resolved that the Bible should be re-established as part of the curriculum in state schools with time being allotted during the day for the reading of portions of the Scriptures without comment by the teacher.
168 *Wisconsin State Journal*, July 23, 1890, p. 1.

workers.[169] Over 800 members of early trade unions joined in this endorsement, when Artisan's Day was celebrated on September 1, 1890 in Sheboygan, an important center of German strength in Wisconsin.[170]

Thus, as the actual election campaigning began, neither Democrats nor Republicans could point to a clear consensus of support for their policy, and both claimed they would be victorious while anxiously attempting to unite diverse religious and secular groups into a solid bloc of votes.

---

169 *Milwaukee Sentinel*, August 28, 1890, p. 9; *Wisconsin State Journal*, August 29, 1890, p. 4.
170 *Milwaukee Sentinel*, September 1, 1890, p. 1.

Reactions of Other Religious Denominations & Nationality Groups
VI

While the reaction of German Lutherans and Catholics to the two platforms was largely inevitable, the attitudes of other religious denominations and nationality groups were not so predictable. The Republican Party leaders and pro-Bennett Law Democrats had quickly noted the fact that most religious groups and even some Lutherans and Catholics found much to commend in the new education law and were not anxious to have it repealed.

Rabbi Sigmund Hecht of Milwaukee's Temple Emanu-El, for example, stated that he could see no actual infringement of the sacred rights of conscience by the law. And yet surely the Jews could not be accused of Know-Nothingism or hostility to freedom of religion, since they had as much to gain as the Catholics from the blessings of liberty. Only recently they had applauded the Supreme Court's Bible-reading decision. Yet, with regard to the Bennett Law, after a careful reading of both the English and German versions, Rabbi Hecht stated that he found in it no attempt to exclude the German language or interfere either with parental rights or parochial schools. In his view, the compulsory education law had been enacted merely because "the government, recognizing the necessity of a physically and mentally well-equipped citizenship, insists upon such measures as will ensure those conditions."[171]

Similar views were held by most English-speaking Protestant groups. Among the most ardent supporters of the Bennett Law were the Episcopalians, Unitarians, and Congregationalists. Prominent ministers from each of these denominations preached throughout the campaign in an effort to counteract other religious opposition to the law. Among these religious groups, one must add, there was also found the greatest fear of "Romanism" in politics. Thus, the Reverend Dean Richmond Babbitt, speaking at St. John's Episcopal Church in Milwaukee, asked: "Have not the people reason to suspect the Romish church when it strikes at their school system, reared at such expense, loved with so much ardor, so useful, so needful, so benevolent?"[172]

Furthermore, the Reverend George Ide, pastor of Milwaukee's Grand Avenue Congregational Church, advised all those without the desire to see their children learn English and become Americans to go back once more beyond the sea. The greatest problem in the

---

171 *Milwaukee Sentinel*, March 22, 1890, p. 3. It is significant that Rabbi Hecht, who could find nothing wrong with the Bennett Law, was a Reform Jew. Like their Protestant and Catholic counterparts, this liberal element in the Hebrew Church welcomed "Americanization," but was met by staunch opposition from conservatives within their own denomination. Rabbi Hecht, himself an immigrant from Hungary, was a figure of some stature in this reform movement, serving as President of the Jewish Relief Society, one of the governors for the Hebrew American College of Cincinnati (a theological seminary founded in 1875 by Rabbi Isaac Wise, a leading Reform Jew), treasurer of the Central Conference of American Jewish Rabbis (founded by Wise in 1889), and a member of the executive committee of the Jewish Sabbath School Union. See Andrew J. Aikens and Lewis A. Proctor, ed.'s, *Men of Progress, Wisconsin* (Milwaukee, 1897), p. 556 and Herberg, pp. 175-177.
172 *Milwaukee Sentinel*, March 17, 1890, p. 2.

United States, he believed, was how to assimilate its heterogeneous population into one society, and the current antagonism toward compulsory school legislation could only be viewed as an example of the stubborn resistance among certain foreign elements to becoming Americanized. Yet, he would point out, the welfare of the country depended upon the character of its citizenship and the strength of its educational system. Thus, quoting Henry Ward Beecher, who had once said: "The children of all nations of the earth go into our common schools, and come out American citizens," the Reverend Ide closed with an urgent appeal to his audience to "Stand by the little school house on the hill."[173]

Similar expressions of concern were voiced by other Congregational ministers during this period of debate. At the same Grand Avenue Church, for example, the Reverend W.G. Gardiner, a visiting clergyman from Michigan, stressed the point that no immigrant had been forced to give up his European home to come to America, and, in any case, the law did not require him to love his native country less, but rather to love his adopted homeland more.[174] Finally, the Ministers' Association, meeting in Milwaukee on September 8, 1890, passed resolutions supporting both the Bennett Law and the study of the English language in all schools.[175]

Some of these ministers, however, were more disturbed by the actions of pastors and priests who abused the freedom of the pulpit by using their religious authority to persuade their congregations how to vote, than by the mere fact that such opposition existed. Criticism of these unethical practices was voiced by the pastor of St.

---

173 *Milwaukee Sentinel*, June 23, 1890, p. 1; *Milwaukee Journal*, September 29, 1890, p. 3; *Wisconsin State Journal*, October 1, 1890, p. 1.
174 *Milwaukee Sentinel*, June 9, 1890, p. 3.
175 *Milwaukee Journal*, September 8, 1890, p. 1.

James Episcopal Church in Milwaukee, while even some Lutheran congregations signed petitions requesting their ministers to cease taking collections for the Democratic Party in their churches on Sunday. To thus drag their religion into "the whirlpool of party politics," they declared, was "a desecration and an indignity."[176]

In a similar vein, the Reverend Theodore Clifton of Milwaukee's Hanover Street Congregational Church, commented that there was no reason why a preacher could not exercise all the privileges of citizenship in voting and working for the party of his choice, but he should realize the proper point to leave the pulpit and work as an ordinary individual.[177] Resolutions concurring in this judgment and confirming support for the State's right to control common school education were passed by a Congregational Convention held at Beloit, Wisconsin, in the fall of 1890.[178]

Among other English-speaking clergymen, a fairly balanced view of the educational question was expressed by the Unitarian minister, J. H. Crooker, of Madison. To begin with, he feared that the papacy might succeed in destroying the public school system. At the same time, however, he was anxious to avoid the stigma of Protestant bigotry and nativism, as he pointed out that there was a difference between the objects of the Roman Catholic hierarchy and ordinary Catholic citizens. He underscored the fact that the American Catholic Church had responded to the spirit of the Age, and its citizens in fact were as loyal and patriotic as any in the United States. Nevertheless, he felt a genuine fear that the church hierarchy's opposition to

---

176 *Milwaukee Sentinel*, March 17, 1890, p. 2; September 24, p. 1.
177 *Milwaukee Sentinel*, April 21, 1890, p. 3.
178 *Wisconsin State Journal*, October 18, 1890, p. 3.

compulsory education would eventually wreck the public school system, thereby destroying the only basis for inculcating the principles of American citizenship.

In the opinion of Reverend Hooker, it was the right and the duty of the state to perpetuate the "American idea" through a system of free secular education. For this reason, he believed, unlike many fellow Protestants, that the recent decision of the Supreme Court on use of Scriptural readings in public schools had been correct, fair to Catholics and agnostics alike. In his view, the Sunday school, the home, and the church were the proper sources of all religious instruction, and in the end, he predicted, the secular public school system would triumph. "The American sentiment," Crooker said, "is an imperial and irresistible power; it will submit to no distinction, it will brook no rival, it will allow no injustice; and while it will protect the Catholic in all his rights and privileges, it will resist and bring to naught any and every opposition which may arise against the organic expression of itself in the public school." Given a fair chance and reasonable support, the public school system would eventually justify its existence by the merit of its work. But in the meantime, it was the duty of clergy and laymen alike to "keep the issue clear and the discussion of it free from passion."[179]

Nevertheless, if one would expect to hear expressions of opposition to anti-Bennett Law proposals more frequently from among Wisconsin's English-speaking Protestant groups, there was also evidence of enough division of opinion among the Lutheran, Catholic, Evangelical, and German Methodist Episcopal churches to bring into serious doubt the belief that this was solely a church-state question. For example, the Lutherans who opposed the law

---

179 *Madison Daily Democrat*, April 1, 1890, p. 4.

continued to have problems with their Scandinavian members and a few Germans who believed in the principles of the statute. Several of their churches even experienced schisms over the issue, and the actual safety of one young German Lutheran pastor was threatened by those in a neighboring congregation who disagreed with his support of the law.[180]

Similar divisions of opinion occurred within the Church of Rome. Thus, in July 1890, a convention of Bohemian Catholics joined with their Polish and Irish brethren, who had already spoken out in favor of the controversial measure, in proclaiming their acceptance of the general tenor and purpose of the act.[181] English-speaking clergy, meanwhile, had formed an American Catholic Clerical Union to represent their views, which frequently diverged from those of the German hierarchy. This union had grown up in Milwaukee in 1887 around the time, and partially in reaction to, Father Abbelen's petition to Rome. Although it attracted to itself mainly Irish and other English-speaking members of the church, a few less conservative German priests, such as John Gmeiner, a former editor of the *Columbia* and a professor at the St. Francis Seminary in Milwaukee, also lent their support. The union's attitude toward Americanization, which was reflected in its support of the aims of the Bennett Law and later in its opposition to Cahenslyism within the

---

180 *Milwaukee Sentinel*, December 5, 1890, p. 8. The Reverend George Kaempflein, who was called to serve as pastor for the newly organized St. John's German Lutheran society in Janesville, formed when a group of Bennett Law supporters left St. Paul's German Lutheran Church, was threatened with violence for his political stand. Several threatening letters were received by the minister after he pointedly refused to preach against the new compulsory education measure, and on a trip to Emerald Grove, Wisconsin, where he hoped to establish another religious society, he felt compelled to take along an armed escort.

181 *Milwaukee Sentinel*, August 1, 1890, p. 4.

church itself, was best summed up in a statement printed in the *Milwaukee Sentinel* on June 20, 1891.

> Resolved that the rights of American Catholics in this country are paramount to all others; that their welfare should first be consulted; that their spiritual wants should first be supplied; that the rights of majorities should be never disregarded, and that in this, our country, foreign customs, foreign ideas, and foreign influences should not be imposed upon us, but rather that all Catholic immigrants to our beloved land should conform to American ways, learn the language of the country and aim to become good, loyal Americans as well as good Catholics.[182]

Among all these groups, in fact—despite earnest attempts by opponents of the law to keep discussion focused on the issue of paternalism—the language problem arose again and again. The Secretary of the Evangelical Association of North America, which met in Milwaukee in April, 1890, expressed the conviction that "Americans should govern America" and defended the proposition that all citizens should be able to speak and write the language of their own country.[183]

In a similar manner, the German Methodists of La Crosse, Oshkosh, Fond du Lac, Appleton, Milwaukee, and other districts passed resolutions endorsing the Wisconsin statute, while several ministers of that denomination wrote the Governor personally in support of his stand.[184] One of these, the Reverend John Schneider of Ripon, read a paper at the Oshkosh conference in which he

---

182 Blied, pp. 39, 59-60. See also Kellogg, "Interview Notes," pp. 2-3.
183 *Milwaukee Sentinel*, April 25, 1890, p. 3.
184 *Milwaukee Sentinel*, May 15, 1890, p. 8; May 25, p. 4; September 3, p. 4. *Milwaukee Journal*, April 1, 1890, p. 4; September 25, p. 1. See also, e.g., Hoard, *Private Letter Books*, 16:490 (a reply to the Rev. O. Roehl, pastor of the German M.E. Church, Manitowoc, Wis.).

contended that the law did not infringe upon parental rights and was important for the future welfare of America. He said:

> I am a German, born in Germany, and I know this: That it is impossible to get that knowledge necessary to vote intelligently in this country, unless you can read and talk the English language and when I know communities of Germans huddled together who teach their children that it is wrong to know the English language and even go so far as to teach them that the devil is in the English language, I say every citizen of this state who wants good and just government should do all they can to uphold the Bennett Law, and all officials who are anxious to prevent this great land from becoming a heterogeneous mass of confusion should see the law is enforced.[185]

Similarly, when religious affiliation is discounted, this same characteristic division of opinion on the law also appears among nationality groups. Moreover, once again the rallying cry of opponents might be to resist paternalism, but an underlying motive clearly involved preservation of their language and customs. Among those who favored the Bennett legislation, some of the staunchest supporters were not surprisingly natives of England, Scotland, and Ireland, for English was already their mother tongue and the Protestants among them seldom supported parochial schools.

Accordingly, the *Western British American*, an influential spokesman for the British interests published in Chicago, called the measure both sound and beneficial, while a recent Scottish immigrant commended its initiators for their wisdom and foresight.[186] Similarly, Thomas Bourke, an Irishman of only

---
185 Quoted in *Wisconsin State Journal*, August 30, 1890, p. 1.
186 Reprinted in *Milwaukee Sentinel*, March 17, 1890, p. 4; quoted in October 21, 1890, p. 5.

one year's residence in America, declared that a warm welcome had awaited the newcomer in this land, and it was, therefore, appropriate that his children should learn the language of the country, so they could take their places alongside children of American parents.[187]

In addition, many Scandinavians were equally concerned about the preservation of the compulsory education statute, not only because of their ordinary affiliation with the Republican Party but because of their desire that their children not be considered "foreigners" in their new home. Thus, Hans Bonlick reported to the editor of the *Sentinel* that the Danes in the area of Waupaca, Farmington, and Lind, where at least one-third of the state's Danish population resided, unanimously favored the Bennett Law.[188]

Moreover, both the *Scandinavian* of Chicago and the *North* published in Minneapolis, the two leading Scandinavian papers of the country, endorsed the measure editorially. The former declared that compulsory education was necessary to prevent widespread illiteracy and was important for children of immigrants, since a lack of English-speaking ability would deter their progress in the new land.[189] The *North*, moreover, denied that the law was an attack upon parochial schools and once more pointed to the English language clause as the real focus of the opposition. Repeal of the Bennett Act, it said, would mean a victory for those who schemed to perpetuate foreign sentiments and language by throwing obstacles in the way of the natural process of Americanization. "For the long and short of the opposition to the Bennett Law lies in the fact that the law obstructs the Germanization of American children.

---
187   *Wisconsin State Journal*, August 30, 1890, p. 4.
188   *Milwaukee Sentinel*, July 7, 1890, p. 4.
189   Editorial of the *Scandinavian* on October 18, 1890, reprinted in *Milwaukee Sentinel*, October 23, 1890, p. 4.

To conceal the true nature of this opposition, *the parental rights doctrine has been trotted out, and the personal liberty dodge drafted into service.*" [Italics theirs.] But the *North* further declared that all true patriotic citizens would soon awaken to this ruse, "rally to the cause of the American school and uphold the supremacy of the English language."[190]

Among German-speaking groups, however, there was considerably less enthusiasm for what was feared to be a form of compulsory nationalization. One notable exception was the liberal Turnverein groups. These organizations, centered in Milwaukee, consisted mainly of the "Intelligentsia" who had fled the unsuccessful 1848 Revolution in their homeland. Liberal in both their political and religious views, they were outspoken advocates of any measure that would insure the integration of their fellow Germans in the community life of their new country. Typical of their beliefs, although actually made in regard to another situation of an earlier date than the Bennett Law crisis, was a statement by Carl Schurz, an eminent leader of this group.

> Let us never forget [he said] that we, as Germans, are not called upon here to form a separate nationality, but rather to contribute to the American nationality the strength there is in us, and in place of our weakness to substitute the strength wherein our fellow Americans excel us and blend it with our wisdom. We should never forget that in the political life of this Republic, we as Germans, have no peculiar interest, but that the universal well-being is ours, also.[191]

---

190 Editorial of the *North*, reprinted in the *Milwaukee Sentinel*, March 22, 1890, p. 9; *Wisconsin State Journal*, September 10, 1890, p. 2. See also letters of reply to messages of support from the editor of the *North* in Hoard, *Private Letter Books*, 16:312 and 18:15, 179.
191 Quoted in Rankin, pp. 128-129.

Another "Forty-Eighter," Christian Essellen, had earlier ventured the opinion that it was a wrong conception of religious tolerance to allow such organizations to take from the state its control over public instruction and afterward to use this power for "selfish, one-sided ecclesiastical purposes."[192] Similar feelings undoubtedly motivated the Milwaukee Turnvereins in decrying the arguments presented in the Bishops' Manifesto of March, 1890 and urging the extension of compulsory English education.[193]

Among the rank and file German-Americans and in such German-language newspapers as the *Milwaukee AbendPost* and *Medford Waldbote*, similar statements now and then appeared. The editor of the *Waldbote*, for example, reminded his readers on several occasions that above everything else they were now American citizens. "All we are, all we possess identifies us with this great country. Our being of German descent, if at all considered, can be but of secondary importance. Whether citizens by birth or not; whether descendants from Irish, Scotch, German, or Russian, we become the moment we take the oath of allegiance a part and parcel of the American people and must serve the national interests, all being subservient to the will of the people."[194]

Kindred expressions of feeling also appeared in letters-to-the-editor columns of local newspapers. Several pointed out that future success in the business world depended on knowledge of the English language, while another saw such education as the key to good citizenship and consequently the basis for the welfare of

---

192 Ernest Bruncken, "The Political Activity of Wisconsin Germans, 1854-60," in Wis. Hist. Soc. *Proceedings*, 1901 (Madison, 1901), pp. 190-211.
193 *Milwaukee Sentinel*, March 13, 1890, p. 1; March 14, p.1; and March 20, p. 1.
194 Translated in *Milwaukee Sentinel*, January 23, 1890, p. 4. See also translation of *Milwaukee AbendPost* editorials in *Milwaukee Sentinel*, May 22, 1890, p. 4; May 24, p. 4; and *Bennett Law Clippings*, I, 40.

both state and nation.[195] One who signed himself simply "German Badger" stressed the fact that this was "not Germany, England, Ireland, Poland, Bohemia or any other country but *America*." If anyone were dissatisfied with the laws of Wisconsin or the United States, he might always return to his homeland. Moreover, he would point out that in deference to large German populations in many areas, their language was taught in public schools. Surely it was not asking too much, he said, also to teach the major language of the country.[196]

Thus, it is apparent that the Bennett Law issue did not create clear-cut divisions among either religious or nationality groups. In both, the leading dissenters were German-speaking, but even within their ranks could be found individuals who believed that accommodation to the new land, although it meant loss of part of their Old-World heritage, was necessary and, indeed, preferable to remaining strangers in their own country.

---

195 *Milwaukee Sentinel*, February 12, 1890, p. 4; March 30, 1890, p. 7. See also the *Sentinel*, July 1, 1890, p. 4; October 21, p. 3. George Oberman, a possible Democratic candidate for governor, put himself out of the running
by stating: "I can't see why Germans should oppose the law. . . . I am a German, and I have pride in the great achievements of the German race in art, science, and literature—but, first of all, I am an American." *Wisconsin State Journal*, October 14, 1890, p. 2.
196 *Milwaukee Sentinel*, October 22, 1890, p. 4.

The Defeat of The Bennett Law

Despite the support of these other national and religious groups, however, Governor Hoard's zeal and confidence in the outcome of the election were not to be vindicated. The remaining weeks between the August political conventions and the fall election brought increasing attempts by the German Catholics and Lutherans, as well as their Democratic allies, to mobilize the votes of Wisconsin's foreign-born population. The Lutherans, in particular, resorted to numerous conventions and meetings to urge their followers to greater efforts in their attempt to elect only those candidates pledged to repeal the Bennett Law. In addition, in order to counter similar efforts by Hoard, the executive anti-Bennett Law committee was instructed to publish pamphlets in English, German, Polish, Norwegian, and Bohemian, setting forth all pertinent objections to the law. Christian Koerner, Conrad Krez, and numerous concerned ministers frequently spoke before meetings of anti-Bennett Law clubs and their sympathizers in order to encourage more active participation in the fight.[197]

---

197   *Milwaukee Journal*, August 30, 1890, p. 1; October 2, p. 1; October 23,

Meanwhile, on August 29, the joint Catholic-Lutheran Anti-Bennett Law Committee passed a resolution declaring support for the Democratic platform and agreed to send out secret circulars to all priests and ministers requesting their aid in defeating the Republicans in November.[198] This was soon done, and reports began appearing in various newspapers that local priests had denounced the law and the Governor from their pulpits, while urging their congregations to vote for Peck and declaring that a vote for Hoard was a sin "beyond forgiveness" or earthly absolution.[199] Even Bishop Katzer of the Green Bay diocese entered the fray. Speaking at an ordination service in St. Mary's Church at Oshkosh, he stated that he "personally and officially, as bishop of the diocese, should consider anyone who did not vote for the repeal of the law a traitor to the Catholic Church."[200]

With the harshness of these attacks and the bitterness engendered on both sides, it is perhaps not surprising that the "Know-Nothing" issue should arise. Even before the heated intensity of the final days of the election campaign caused individuals to become less judicious in their statements, charges of nativism had appeared in speeches by representatives of both factions.[201]

---

p. 4. *Milwaukee Sentinel*, August 21, 1890, p. 2; September 16, p. 1; September 20, p. 1; September 25, p. 1; October 6, p. 1; October 17, p. 2.
198   *Milwaukee Sentinel*, August 30, 1890, p. 1; September 19, p. 1 (translation of the Catholic circular). See also *Wisconsin State Journal*, September 19, 1890, p. 1; September 20, p. 2.
199   *Milwaukee Sentinel*, October 27, 1890, pp. 3-4; October 28, p. 2; November 3, p. 8. These issues of the *Sentinel* contain reports of such statements by Catholic clergymen in Rhinelander, Eau Claire, Watertown, Oshkosh, and other towns throughout the state.
200   Quoted in *Milwaukee Sentinel*, October 28, 1890, p. 2.
201   After the municipal election in Milwaukee in the spring of 1890, articles appearing in the *St. Louis Republic, St. Paul Globe, Charleston News and Courier, Boston Globe,* and other papers charged that the Bennett Law movement had originated in Boston and was a primary example of Puritan intolerance. Simi-

In actuality, the original American, or Know-Nothing, Party was no longer in existence, having dwindled away rapidly after its disastrous defeat in the presidential election of 1856. However, another secret nativist organization, founded in 1887 by Henry F. Bowers of Clinton, Iowa and named the American Protective Association (A.P.A.), had since taken up the anti-Catholic, anti-immigrant crusade.

Although its strength was never great in Wisconsin, and no evidence of a connection between that movement and the passage of the 1889 compulsory education act exists, German Catholics in the state cast a wary eye on the secret society and found in its announced goals the source for much of the motivation of pro-Bennett Law forces.[202] But, they warned, they were "'on the watch'" and would "'know how to thwart the black schemes of the Know-Nothings if they actually attempt their realization.'"[203]

larly, the *Milwaukee Journal* stated that the law was an indication that a "new know-nothingism" had grown up in Wisconsin, and Christian Koerner warned in a speech to an anti-Bennett Law meeting at Oshkosh on October 9, 1890, that they "must not cease until we have disposed of the spirit of Knownothingism completely in our state." See *Milwaukee Sentinel*, October 14, 1890, p. 4. Even some modern religious historians like August Stellhorn have found the seeds of nativism implanted in the Bennett enactment. Indeed, a number of textbook authors have stated that the Wisconsin law, like that passed in Oregon in 1922, was deliberately aimed at destroying the Catholic parochial school system. On the basis of the evidence available, however, the conclusion must be that such allegations are in error. If religious or national prejudice motivated any supporters of the law, it was not the reason for its originally having been written and passed.

202   For a good general discussion of the nativist movement in America during the 19th century, see John Higham, *Strangers in the Land* (New Brunswick, N.J., 1955). Humphrey J. Desmond, in *The A.P.A. Movement, A Sketch* (Washington, 1912) deals with the most prominent movement in the Middle West. For a Catholic view of the A.P.A. and its relation to school legislation in Illinois and Wisconsin, see also Thomas J. Jenkins, "A.P.A. Conspirators," *Catholic World*, LVII (1893), 685-693.

203   Editorial from *Der Herold*, translated in *Milwaukee Sentinel*, October 16, 1889, p. 2.

The Republicans, in turn, protested that they were the victims of "inverted know-nothingism" as their opponents sought to promote a "Germanism" separate from the other nationality groups in America. As proof of their claims, they pointed to the often intemperate remarks of Koerner and Krez, who were constantly urging their followers to greater efforts against the law in the name of the Fatherland.[204]

Yet despite the multitude of charges made against both sides, evidence for a full-scale campaign of nativism in Wisconsin is surprisingly scarce. The *America*, a propaganda sheet published in Chicago by the A.P.A., did print several articles on the Bennett Law, in which it trumpeted its usual catch-phrase, "America is for Americans," and proclaimed that such legislation was a "beacon light of patriotic hope" for the future greatness of the nation.[205] In addition, on September 18, 1890, the *Milwaukee Journal* printed an unsubstantiated report that the City's Republican League was planning to organize Know-Nothing clubs and would soon issue a circular denouncing the invasion of the public school system by promoters of Catholicism and parochial schools.[206]

There was also a minor uproar over an anti-Catholic cartoon, taken from the July issue of the *Pauline Propaganda Monthly* published in Boston, which featured the Pope in the form of an alligator, who in creeping up towards a schoolhouse was intercepted by the Goddess of Liberty with sword in hand. Underneath was printed the admonition: "Dump the Roman

---

204 This term was used to describe the violent anti-Bennett Law speech made by Colonel Krez at Milwaukee on December 27, 1889. See editorial of the *Manitowoc Pilot*, in *Bennett Law Clippings*, I, 67.
205 Duane Mowry, "The Bennett Law" in *America*, January 30, 1890, on file in *Bound Bennett Law Pamphlets*.
206 *Milwaukee Journal*, September 18, 1890, p. 1.

reptiles out of the cradle of liberty and let no foreign usurpers rule the United States."[207]

The Democrats charged that their political opponents were responsible for circulating the cartoon throughout the state. The Republicans, however, not only indignantly denied the allegation but also claimed that by circulating thousands of copies of the cartoon as "evidence" for that accusation, the members of the Catholic anti-Bennett Law Committee had themselves played into the hands of Boston fanatics and had done more harm to their religion than whoever was responsible for spreading the few original copies. In Republican eyes, it was in fact "a shameful trick" perpetrated by those who cared more for a Democratic victory in the next election than their own church.[208]

On the other hand, the Republicans were equally incensed over a Democratic cartoon showing a headsman's block on which was lying a woman, blindfolded, labeled "private schools" and over whom the headsman (Governor Hoard) stood with an axe labeled "The Bennett Law." In the same scene, Horace Rublee, editor of the *Sentinel*, was shown on a ladder, holding a basket in which to catch the head; Henry Payne, Republican campaign manager, whetted the edge of the Bennett Law axe with the party platform; and Charles Felker, chairman of the Democratic Bennett Law League, appeared as a clown labeled "Rum, Romanism, and Rebellion Felker."[209] Furthermore, Republicans also objected to

---

207 *Milwaukee Journal*, October 9, 1980, p. 3. See also a letter from J.C. Ludwig, chairman of the Catholic Anti-Bennett Committee, charging that the Republicans were responsible for circulating the cartoon, in *Milwaukee Sentinel*, October 11, 1890, p. 4.
208 *Milwaukee Sentinel*, October 13, 1890, p. 4; *Wisconsin State Journal*, October 14, 1890, p. 4.
209 Editorial from the *Portage Register*, reprinted in *Milwaukee Sentinel*, October 27, 1890, p. 4.

such repeated references to the governor as a "narrow-hearted hater of Germans and enemy of religion."[210]

In actuality, however, these flare-ups were minor, and there was in the election campaign very little of the hysterical and vitriolic speech-making such as characterized the Boston Know-Nothing campaigns in the 1850s. Some Protestant clergymen undoubtedly overstepped the bounds of fairness at times in denouncing possible "Romanist" schemes. Yet, Colonel Krez was guilty of making equally venomous attacks against "Anglo-Americans" on behalf of German Catholics and Lutherans. Nevertheless, more important was the fact that a substantial number of influential spokesmen for both sides realized the dangers of anti-religious and nativistic battles in politics and strove to prevent the main issue from degenerating to such a level. In the one instance where a suggestion was made to the governor that he circulate a speech containing anti-Catholic remarks, it was instantly vetoed, while even *Der Herold*, a leading German-language opposition paper, apologized for some of the more vituperative comments of Colonel Krez.[211]

In short, while the record is not entirely clean on either side, there was far less evidence for religious and nationalistic prejudice than might be expected in view of the nature of the controversy. It is certainly not fair to say, as even some modern church historians have done, that the entire campaign constituted an attempt by the state to subvert religious liberty and rights of conscience. It was a church-state controversy, but the very strong and very significant undertones resulting from the difficulties faced by immigrant

---

210 Translation from the *Seebote*, in *Milwaukee Sentinel*, October 16, 1890, p. 4.
211 Hoard, *Private Letter Books*, 17:107. The *Milwaukee Sentinel* acknowledged *Der Harold*'s apologies for Krez's speech in the editorial. See *Bennett Law Clippings*, I, 66.

churches in accommodating their institutions to the American situation made it a much more complex phenomenon than it is usually credited as being. Only in an awareness of this complexity, however, can the development of the Bennett Law into an election issue be fully understood.

Meanwhile, at the same time that the Catholics and Lutherans were busily engaged in a last-minute drive for victory, the two main political parties were also actively preparing for the November 4 election day. The Democrats had adopted a campaign banner with an extract from Wisconsin's constitution, declaring the right of every man to worship according to his conscience,[212] and they continued to stump the state with speeches echoing this sentiment and reiterating the charges of state interference and paternalism.

Roger Q. Mills, a Democratic U.S. Representative from Texas, addressed a gathering in Racine on September 21, 1890, and called the law an attack against liberty and the educational principles laid down by Jefferson. Quoting from the Scriptures, he stated flatly that it was the parent, not the Republican legislature of Wisconsin, who had received God's command to "train the child up in the way he shall go." Thus, he urged children to obey their fathers in this manner and not the governor. The *Chicago Tribune* denounced Mills' speech as an exhibition of "southern impudence" by a man who could not possibly understand the principle of the question as it applied to Wisconsin.[213] Nevertheless, Colonel William F. Vilas and other Democrats not only continued this line of argument before various groups, but also hammered at the question of just why it should make any difference whether a child

---

212 *Wisconsin State Journal*, September 18, 1890, p. 1.
213 *Milwaukee Journal*, September 22, 1890, p. 1; September 23, p. 1; October 3, p. 4. *Wisconsin State Journal*, September 25, 1890, pp. 1-2.

said "*zwei und zwei machen vier*" or "two and two make four."[214] It was apparent that neither side was going to rest before the final votes were counted.

Thus, in these last weeks before the election, the Republicans were equally active in declaring their position on the law. A most potent argument for them was their claim that the Bennett Law, which had now been in effect for one year, had actually increased attendance in public, *as well as private*, schools by substantial numbers, although there had been neither prosecutions of individuals[215] nor interference with the management of denominational schools. In short, supporters of the law believed it had proven its effectiveness without resulting in any of the dire consequences predicted by its critics.

Thus, a report issued by the Superintendent of Schools for Dane County in 1890 showed that in that one district alone, there had been registered a net increase of 349 pupils in attendance at some school, or a 5 percent gain over the preceding year. Furthermore, in contradiction of church fears, this gain represented only a three and a third (3-1/3) percent increase in public school attendance, but a sixty and two-thirds (60-2/3) percent increase for all private schools.[216] In the state as a whole, Superintendent Thayer reported that since the Bennett Law went into effect, the percentage of children between the ages of 7 and 14 who did not attend any

---

214 *Wisconsin State Journal*, October 15, 1890, p. 1; October 30, p. 2.
215 A suit brought by the Sullivan school board of Jefferson County in May against William Wendt, Charles Moods, and Fred Keller for non-compliance with the Bennett Law was dropped on June 5, 1890. The board reportedly doubted the strength of the new law and, therefore, declined to proceed with the case. See *Milwaukee Journal*, May 23, 1890, p. 1; June 5, p. 1.
216 "Annual Report of the Superintendent of the First Dane County District," printed in the *Wisconsin State Journal*, October 31, 1890, p. 4; January 26, 1891, p. 1.

school had dropped from 14.3 percent in 1889 to 10.6 percent in 1890. In other words, an additional 20,235 children were currently attending some school, public or private. Yet on the basis of past statistics, gains due to normal increases in the school-age population would have accounted for only 9,257 of these. Thus, it was believed, 11,102 children had received 12 weeks or more of schooling in 1889, who—except for the compulsory education law—would not have attended any school whatsoever.[217] See Table 3.

Armed with these figures, the Republicans now prepared to take their case before the people in an effort to gain popular acceptance for the necessity of the Bennett Law. An interesting development of their campaign, although it had little bearing on the actual outcome at the polls, was the concern aroused in the mind of one civil service commissioner in Washington, D.C. In a long letter to the editor of the *Wisconsin State Journal* indicative of his later strong nationalism as president, Theodore Roosevelt wrote that his federal service office might debar his active participation in the election campaign, but he nonetheless felt it was his duty as a patriotic American to express his conviction that all citizens should have a knowledge of their country's language so that they could understand its laws and institutions. It was essential, he believed, that a child should grow up to be "an American, and not merely a foreigner who happens to have been born in America." In the latter case, youngsters would cease to be Europeans without becoming true citizens of their new country, and thus they would soon have no proper place in either land.

---

217 "Biennial Report of the State Superintendent of Wisconsin for the Two Years Ending June 30, 1890," in *Wisconsin Governor's Message and Accompanying Documents*, I (Madison, 1891), p.3. Reprinted in Hoard, *Private Letter Books*, 18:112-113. See also *Wisconsin State Journal*, October 8, 1890, p. 1 and *Milwaukee Sentinel*, October 11, 1890, p. 8.

At the same time, however, Roosevelt was clear that he did not wish to imply support for the bigoted nativists who saw the immigrant as a threat to society. In fact, he simply had no patience with any person who spoke of himself habitually as an American with qualifying prefix, whether this was native-American, German-American, Irish-American, or any other. "The term American," he said, "is quite broad enough to cover us all; and no man is worth his salt, or has any business to continue to live in this country, unless he is proudly conscious of the fact that there is no freeman in the world who can aspire to a prouder title than that of American. Americanism is a question of spirit, purpose, belief, and conviction; not of creed or birthplace."[218]

Meanwhile, within the state, Republicans had joined forces with the newly organized Democratic Bennett Law League. As early as April 1890, rumors had been circulating that hinted at a possible fusion ticket between the Republicans and dissident elements of the Democratic Party. This ticket, it was believed, would be headed by Governor Hoard with Charles W. Felker, an Oshkosh Democrat, for attorney general and a balance between parties for other offices.[219] Although such a ticket never actually materialized, by September a Democratic Bennett Law League had been founded, and Republican papers were gleefully reporting desertions from the ranks of their opponents.[220] These Democrats urged possible sympathizers not to fear the name of "bolter" or feel that they were betraying their former principles by their stand, for they said, "there are times when blind allegiance to party leaders becomes treason

---

218   Letter from Theodore Roosevelt, dated October 8, 1890, in *Wisconsin State Journal*, October 18, 1890, p. 1.
219   *Madison Daily Democrat*, April 20, 1890, p. 1.
220   *Wisconsin State Journal*, September 1, 1890, p. 1; September 4, p. 4.

to party, to the state, to reason, and to conscience." Clearly, in their eyes such a time was the present, for after examining the primary objections to the law, League members had concluded that they were groundless and that the primary motive for repeal centered in the opposition of some German church groups to the teaching of English.

It was, in the opinion of these members, not a question of state interference with the rights and liberties of its citizens, but rather the encroachment of the churches on the functions and power of the state.[221] In this, moreover, the Democratic "bosses" were just as much to blame, for they were motivated in their actions by the desire for political spoil. Charles Felker, chairman of the Democratic Bennett Law Committee, charged that Peck and Vilas had, for a handful of votes, sacrificed principle, patriotism, and the honorable traditions of their party.[222]

"Do you agree to this?" asked a League bulletin. "Will you not leave this free institution under which you live to your children and grandchildren unharmed? If you would not deliver the politics of our state into the hands of a fanatic clergy; if you as a free citizen will preserve the sovereign rights of the state, then it is indifferent whether you are Republican, Democrat, Lutheran, Catholic, German, Irish, or American by birth, but as a patriotic citizen of our beautiful commonwealth, you have to take up the fight against the enemy and cast your vote in November against the democratic candidates for state offices."[223]

---

221 "Address of the Democratic Bennett Law League" (Milwaukee, 1890), pp. 1, 7, 9 [pamphlet in possession of Wis. State Hist. Soc.]. A second address was reprinted in *Wisconsin State Journal*, September 30, 1890, p. 1.
222 *Wisconsin State Journal*, October 20, 1890, p. 1.
223 The second address of the Bennett Law League in *Wisconsin State Journal*, September 30, 1890, p. 1.

At the same time that the Democratic Bennett Law League was thus appealing to members of its own party, the headquarters of the Republican State Central Committee issued its own position statement to voters. In it, they presented the case for the existence of such a law and for the last time denied that any religious or national prejudices had motivated their support of it. The Bennett Law, Republicans repeated, was both necessary and just, and they were certain that the voters would render a verdict favorable to their cause.[224] On this note, they rested their case and prepared for the balloting.

Election Day, November 4, 1890, proved clear and sunny. Good weather and the great interest engendered by the months of debating seemed bound to insure a fine turnout of voters. In addition, this was a congressional election year, and economic issues resulting from the recently enacted McKinley tariff had yet to be decided, although its coverage in state newspapers had been considerably less intensive than the educational controversy. Republicans, despite evidence of some desertions from party ranks by German Lutherans, remained confident of victory. Indeed, one Republican journalist who campaigned for the governor in the Lake Shore counties later recalled that the party fully expected to poll a plurality of at least 100,000 votes for Hoard.[225] Not even the early returns dampened their optimism. Milwaukee was lost to the Democrats, but this could have been expected in view of the large preponderance of Germans in the population and the spring municipal victory of George Peck. The governor, who had stumped the state in the autumn of 1889 speaking at country fairs and agricultural expositions, insisted that returns from the rural districts would uphold the principle of the Bennett Law.

---

224 *Wisconsin State Journal*, October 31, 1890, p. 1.
225 Kellogg, "The Bennett Law," p. 23 (footnote).

As to potential blocs of religious voters, there had long been a divergence of opinion in Republican ranks. Hoard himself staunchly maintained that the German Lutheran vote did not exceed 7,000, and most of these, he believed, contrary to the opinion of other party leaders, were Democrats. On the basis of the last election returns, that would still leave 168,000 votes in the Republican fold.[226] Furthermore, even if all 7,000 German Lutherans deserted the ranks, the party could still win the election, since it could count on support from both Prohibitionists, numbering 14,000, and at least 10,000 Laborites. Then, of course, there would very likely be defections from the ranks of their opponents, as witnessed by the growth of the Democratic Bennett Law League.[227] In short, in the governor's eyes, the outlook for victory was extremely hopeful.

On the other hand, Jeremiah Rusk and other professional politicians maintained just as strongly that the true number of German Lutherans whose support would go to anti-Bennett Law candidates was closer to 40,000, and almost all of these had formerly been Republicans. Should such a large bloc of support be alienated, Rusk warned, the party would not only lose the election, but also their pre-eminent position in Wisconsin state politics for years to come.[228]

In actual fact, the results of the election were to bear out the predictions of the most pessimistic Republican Party members. The German Lutherans and Catholics were out in force, often coming to the polls in clearly recognizable groups. In the final analysis, even many Scandinavians, Poles, and Bohemians joined

---
226 Letter to Congressman Myron McCord in Hoard, *Private Letter Books*, 16:995. See also *ibid.*, pp. 478-481.
227 Hoard, *Private Letter Books*, 16:316.
228 Rusk, *Letters of Jeremiah Rusk to Henry Casson*, 4:464-465.

in protest against the law. Feelings ran so high that Governor Hoard was hissed and booed when he tried to speak to a gathering at Hales Corners, just outside Milwaukee, until he could no longer continue. Another mob was responsible for kicking in the door to his home.[229] Finally, it was also revealed by the governor after the election that in the final weeks of the campaign there had even been a plot to take his life.[230]

Nevertheless, such violent forms of opposition seemed hardly necessary later in view of the actual election returns. Peck polled 160,388 votes, or a total of 28,320 more than his opponent's 132,068.[231] Nor did the landslide end with the governorship. As the editor of the *Wisconsin State Journal* lamented several days after the election, "the simple fact is the Republican Party of Wisconsin is for the time being snowed under."[232] The Democrats carried both houses of the State Legislature, with a wide majority in the Assembly and all but two of the contested seats in the Senate. On a national level, both Senator John Spooner and Congressman Robert La Follette were defeated. Indeed, eight of the nine Congressmen elected to office in 1890 were

---

229   *Milwaukee Sentinel*, November 4-6, 1890, pp. 1, 4.
230   *Milwaukee Journal*, November 6, 1890, p. 1. After the election, the Governor revealed that in the latter days of the campaign, he had received an anonymous letter stating that five Catholics were plotting to take his life. The *Journal* denounced Hoard for discussing the plot and thereby slandering the fair name of the state. In 1918, in his interview with Dr. Kellogg (see her notes, pp. 5-6), the former governor gave this account of what had transpired. While campaigning, he said, he had received an anonymous letter stating that a certain man was waiting for a chance to murder him. Hoard did in fact begin to notice in his audiences a man who seemed to follow him closely. In Sheboygan, the same man followed him on a walk. Turning and facing him, Governor Hoard, in a bluff, stated that he knew who he was and who had sent him. At that, the man ran off and did not bother him again.
231   See "Election Statistics" in *Wisconsin Blue Book, 1891*, pp. 256-257.
232   *Wisconsin State Journal*, November 6, 1890, p. 1.

Democrats.²³³ Quite obviously, the Republican Party had been completely and thoroughly overwhelmed in all its political contests.

Governor Hoard's reaction to this stunning defeat was not inconsistent with his earlier stand on principle, but it was undoubtedly of little comfort to his fellow party leaders. "I am content," he said, "so far as I am personally concerned. More than a year and a half ago I was willing to step out of the office if the people wished it, rather than sacrifice my honest convictions of duty. I saw my duty, I have performed it to the best of my ability, and I am willing to abide by the consequences."²³⁴ To all expressions of condolence, he offered no regrets but reiterated his belief that conscience had required the stand he had taken. Like Henry Clay, he wrote, he "had rather be right than President."²³⁵

At the same time, however, the governor refused to believe that the issue had been permanently settled. Rather, the election defeat

---

233   *Wisconsin Blue Book, 1891*, pp. 202-253, 255-263, 303-312, 490-494. Of all the Republican candidates for Congress, only Nils P. Haugen, a popular Norwegian-American, was re-elected. Although John C. Spooner was not defeated directly by the voters, since the Seventeenth Amendment had not yet been ratified, the plurality received by the Democrats in both houses of the state legislature meant that he would not be reappointed for another term. In the contest for state assembly seats, Michael J. Bennett, whose name was attached to the now famous but ill-fated compulsory education law, was defeated by his Democratic opponent by a margin of 153 votes out of a total of 2,376 ballots cast. In 1888, Bennett's own plurality had been 160 votes. After his defeat in 1890, Bennett seems to have faded into political obscurity. On the other hand, Conrad Krez, outspoken German critic of the Bennett Law and comic poet of the campaign, won a seat in the 1890 assembly by defeating the Republican nominee by a total of 925 votes. During his two-year term, Krez served on the Judiciary Committee, and in 1892, he was chosen by the voters for the position of city attorney of Milwaukee. See Berryman, p. 548, and *Wisconsin Blue Book, 1891*, pp. 308, 596.
234   Interview quoted in *Wisconsin State Journal*, November 5, 1890, p. 1.
235   Letter to the Reverend W.J. McKay of Sparta, Wisconsin, dated November 10, 1890, in Hoard, *Private Letter Books*, 18:325-326. Other letters in this volume contain the same expressions of conviction that he had done his duty and acted rightly according to his conscience.

seemed to him merely to be a Bull Run, with Appomattox yet to come. Thus, although the progress of the "little school house" had been temporarily checked, one should not lose heart. In the opinion of Hoard, the Bennett Law was both necessary and constitutional, and as he left office, he had no fear that his stand would not one day be vindicated.[236]

To other Republicans, however, belonged the task of analyzing the reasons for defeat and determining the means to recoup party losses in the next election. Initial reaction was one of shock and dismay at the extent of the landslide. "Yesterday was Black Friday for the Republican Party of Wisconsin," said the editor of the *Beloit Free Press*, while an Ashland paper commented: "The state of Wisconsin is in deep disgrace today—humiliated, branded un-American and unpatriotic before the nation. The schoolhouse may win two years from now if there is any latent manhood in American character, but it will be many years before the stain of shame is effaced."[237]

Bigotry and superstition were blamed for the disastrous defeat, and fears were expressed that fanatical ecclesiastics would take advantage of their victory to set up a clerical or church party. "Priestcraft has shown its ugly head," said one Republican after the election, "and the conscienceless politician is in his glory when he can egg on and take advantage of prejudice."[238]

---

236 Letter to John Throne of Watertown, Wisconsin, November 7, 1890, in Hoard, *Private Letter Books*, 18:264.
237 Quoted in the *Milwaukee Journal*, November 17, 1890, p. 8. The article contains numerous excerpts from Republican journals from the entire state on the causes and results of their party's election defeat.
238 Editorial from the *Oshkosh Northwestern*, reprinted in *Wisconsin State Journal*, November 11, 1890, p. 2. The *Medford Star and News* commented glumly: "It has been supposed that Henry M. Stanley was doing the world a service by explorations 'in darkest Africa,' where the people are supposed to be enshrouded in black ignorance. Mr. Stanley has wasted his time, for there

Surprisingly enough, however, there was actually some question concerning the importance of the Bennett Law in causing such an overwhelming defeat. Democrats, of course, like many Republicans,[239] believed that the compulsory education law was the primary factor involved. "I am gratified at the Democratic victory," said Joseph Donally in an interview for the *Milwaukee Sentinel*. "It is a protest against legislative intermeddling with matters of conscience. It is a rebuke to religious intolerance. . . . Bigotry has a black eye, liberality a laurel wreath. God bless all our schools." At the same time, normally outspoken critic Conrad Krez said simply: "I have nothing to say except that the Lord was registered at every poll."[240] Nevertheless, some Republicans, including Congressman Haugen and Governor Hoard himself, believed that another issue, namely the McKinley tariff, had been

---

is work for him in Wisconsin, where the people have decided against the best compulsory education law ever presented to any people. Sectarian hate has fostered this outcome, and ecclesiastics, for the first time in the history of the state, took an active part in politics, holding political meetings on Sunday and instructing their congregations how they should vote. . . . The Lutheran and Catholic churches take their places permanently as political forces in this state, and one taste of power will only aggravate the desire to rule." Quoted in *Milwaukee Journal*, November 17, 1890, p. 4.

239 Although Governor Hoard saw other reasons besides the Bennett Law for the overwhelming defeat of the party, other Republicans believed this had been without question the deciding factor in the election outcome. George Hazelton, a former congressman, remarked that "'Hoard with his school question drove all the Lutherans away from our party, the German Lutherans especially, and the Norwegians stayed away from the polls.'" Spooner, who was personally bitter against the governor for the loss of his Senate seat, declared that the Republican Party had "'gone to hell through his stupidity.'" It was, he said, the school law that caused it all, "'a silly, sentimental and damned useless abstraction, foisted upon us by a self-righteous demagogue.'" Indeed, his only consolation was that Hoard had fallen with the rest. See Fowler, pp. 152-153. A post-election interview with Spooner may also be found in the *Milwaukee Sentinel*, November 13, 1890, p. 2.

240 Interview with A.C. Brazee and other Republican and Democratic politicians in the *Milwaukee Sentinel*, November 6, 1890, p. 4.

just as decisive in determining the final outcome of the election.[241] Nor, in actuality, can this contention be altogether discounted.

In 1890, Wisconsin's election results were not atypical for the nation as a whole. Throughout the country, the Republican Party suffered enormous losses in the Congressional elections. In the U.S. Senate, for example, their majority was reduced to 8, while in the House they managed to secure only 88 seats in comparison with 235 for the Democrats and 9 for the Alliance-Populists. Notable, too, was the defeat of Congressman William McKinley, author of the bill, in his own state of Ohio. Political analysts credited this overwhelming defeat of the Republican Party to the popular revulsion against high tariff duties, which their opponents pictured as the main reason for rising living costs, and to a widespread uneasiness over the condition and direction of the nation's economy.[242]

Governor Hoard and some of his followers believed that this concern with the tariff had also accounted for an unusual phenomenon in the state elections—that is, the large number of "stay-at-home" Republicans who had not voted at all.[243] Official

---

241   Nils P. Haugen, *Pioneer and Political Reminiscences* (Evansville, Wis., 1929), p. 95. See Hoard's letter to Rasmus B. Anderson dated December 23, 1915, published in Anderson, *Life Story*, pp. 672-675 (Appendix). The original copy, typewritten and signed by the governor, can be found in Hoard's *Private Papers* in the Wisconsin State Historical Society at Madison. Other letters written at the time of the controversy also contain this observation by the governor regarding the effect of the McKinley bill on the outcome of the 1890 election. See, e.g., Letter to Fred Schuette of Manitowoc, Wis., November 11, 1890, in Hoard, *Private Letter Books*, 18:344-345.

242   National election results can be found in any Wisconsin newspaper. See, e.g., *Wisconsin State Journal*, November 5, 1890, p. 1. Note also the discussion in T. Harry Williams, Richard Current, and Frank Freidel, *A History of the United States [since 1865]* (New York, 1960), p. 199.

243   Governor Hoard made this claim in an interview with a reporter for the *Milwaukee Sentinel*, November 7, 1890, p. 1. Republican journals through-

returns showed an astonishing decrease in the Republican vote since the previous election. See Table 4. An estimate based on the returns of nearly 500 towns indicated that one out of every four voters in 1888 had not gone to the polls for the 1890 election. In Eau Claire County, for example, 1,382 out of 6,267 failed to vote; in Sauk, 1,257 out of 6,626; in Marinette, 1,127 out of 3,891; in Burnett, 192 out of 788; in Pepin, 411 out of 1,562; and in Bayfield, 1,129 out of 2,976.[244] If the 1,300 Republicans who neglected their duty in Dane County had voted, it was estimated that Congressman Robert La Follette would have won by a plurality of 700 votes, instead of going down to defeat as he actually did.[245]

In the state as a whole, although from five- to eight-thousand Democrats gave their support to Hoard, nearly 45,000 Republicans failed to go to the polls. At the same time, Peck's total vote was only about 5,000 more than that of his party's previous candidate. In short, for whatever reason—the tariff question, disquiet over their party's stand on the educational issue, apathy, confusion over the Australian ballot rule which went into effect for the first time that year, or even (as some commentators believed) the desire of farmers to take advantage of good plowing weather—approximately 40,000 Wisconsin voters did not go to the polls in 1890.[246]

---

out the state also commented repeatedly on this widespread absence from the polls of their party's voters.
244 *Milwaukee Sentinel*, November 7, 1890, p. 1.
245 *Wisconsin State Journal*, November 6, 1890, p. 4. See also Hoard, *Private Letter Books*, 18:272-273.
246 Many journals, and the Governor himself, put the total number of "stay-at-home" Republicans as high as fifty or sixty thousand. See, e.g., *Wisconsin State Journal*, November 7, 1890, p. 1. Governor Hoard, in addition to stressing the importance of the McKinley bill in keeping party voters away from the polls, also blamed to some extent overconfidence, the good weather that

Although it is difficult, of course, to state absolutely which of these factors proved most important in causing such widespread absence from the polls, it is equally hard to distinguish with certainty the effect of the two main issues on the minds of those who actually did vote in the election. This is especially true, since a large proportion of the Germans were farmers and therefore concerned with the outcome of both the Bennett Law and the McKinley tariff questions. Despite the inconclusiveness of any such speculation, however, it appears valid to say that for the Germans the deciding factor in determining their vote was the Bennett Law problem.

The City of Milwaukee, which played a very great part in determining the election outcome by its overwhelming support of Peck, was after all an urban manufacturing center, normally Republican in its allegiance and, therefore, unlikely to so radically alter its voting patterns just to oppose a tariff designed to protect its own developing industry. Furthermore, in all the pre- and post-election comments of German political and religious leaders, as well as in German-language newspaper editorials, virtually the only topic of discussion was the Bennett Law.

On the other hand, among the large numbers of English-speaking Republicans who favored the compulsory education measure but who either voted against Hoard or stayed away from the polls entirely, the economic issue undoubtedly played a significant role in influencing their decision. In the end, however, as the following

---

enabled farmers to catch up on fall plowing, and the Cooper Law. The latter measure put into effect for the first time that year, required a secret ballot. This, combined with the long list of party officers, confused many voters, Governor Hoard commented in the interview with Dr. Kellogg. In fact, he said, "Henry Casson made an estimate that if everyone who had voted for Hoard had also voted for a Republican senator and representative, there would have been a seventeen majority for that party in each house, and Spooner would have been returned to the U.S. Senate instead of Vilas." See Kellogg, *Interview Notes*, p. 2.

comparative analysis of state election statistics for the years 1886 to 1894 will reveal, the most important fact was that the German vote did successfully defeat Governor Hoard for re-election in 1890. For the purposes of this analysis, the author has divided the total number of Wisconsin counties into four groups according to the percentage of Germans in their populations. These percentages are based on statistics provided in the U.S. Census of 1880. The four categories represent counties with a German population of less than 8 percent, 8 to 10 percent, 9 to 14 percent, or 15 to 30 percent of the total.[247] See Table 5.

In reviewing these statistics, one would naturally expect on the basis of past discussion to find the greatest number of votes against Hoard registered in counties with the highest percentage of Germans in the total population. This, in fact, is what actually occurred. Thus, although eight of the eighteen counties in the 15-to-30 percent group gave their votes to the Republican candidates for governor in 1886 and 1888, all eighteen of them voted against Hoard in 1890. In addition, Sheboygan, which had remained Democratic in both earlier elections, raised its margin of victory by 1,595 votes, while others showed increases almost as high.

Of all these counties, however, Milwaukee with the greatest number of Germans in the state provided the most significant voting statistics. For example, this one county, which had given Hoard and Rusk a plurality of two to three thousand votes in the two previous elections, suddenly in 1890 served George Peck with an astounding 6,207 vote margin of victory. Moreover, in the City of Milwaukee itself the Democratic candidate won by a plurality

---

247 The divisions of counties were based on the census information of 1880 and are the same as those shown on the maps in Kate Everest, "How Wisconsin Came By Its Large German Element," p. 304f. and Kellogg, "The Bennett Law," p.6.

of 5,299. The significance of these figures becomes even clearer when it is recalled that the Democrats in 1890 registered only a small increase of about 5,000 votes over their previous record in 1888. Yet this city, which only two years before had provided Hoard with a plurality of 2,154 now gave him 5,299 fewer votes than his Democratic rival, George Peck.

The importance of this reversal of strength to the outcome of the election is obvious. Nevertheless, one must also note that by 1892 Peck's margin had dwindled to only 892 votes, and two years afterward his opponent, William B. Upham, received an astonishing 6,333 vote plurality. Similarly, in that year, Milwaukee County as a whole swung back into the Republican camp, along with eight other counties, one of which had voted Democratic ever since 1886.

Among the nine counties that numbered 11 to 14 percent of its population with those of German extraction, a similar pattern emerged. Seven of these had voted for Hoard in the election of 1888. Yet, two years later only one of them continued to do so, and his plurality there had dropped from 854 to 209. Nevertheless, by 1894, all except Kewaunee once more gave their support to the Republican candidate. Thus, as with the first group of counties, the issue—whether Bennett Law or McKinley tariff—which swayed a majority of votes in 1890 seemingly no longer applied in 1894, and as a result a particular nationality trend was no longer evident.

In turning to the areas of the state where the German population was smaller, one discovers that although these voting patterns become less pronounced, they are nonetheless still apparent. For example, in 1888 eight of the nine counties classified in the 8- to 10-percent bracket voted for Governor Hoard, while in 1890 only four continued to do so. Furthermore, among these four, the Republican plurality in Ashland County dropped from 655 to 32;

in Grant, from 857 to 166; in Waupaca, from 1,605 to 450; and in Waushara, from 1,600 to 821. The least amount of switching in party allegiance occurred, not surprisingly, in the 32 counties where Germans numbered less than 8 percent of the population. Indeed, of these, only ten voted for Peck in 1890, and generally by small margins. Moreover, two of them—Langlade and Oneida—had been Democratic in 1888.

It is interesting to note also that in many of these counties—Barron, Bayfield, Douglas, Polk, and Vernon, to name a few—Scandinavians were the predominant immigrant group. Despite the fact that many Lutherans opposed the Bennett Law, the Swedish, Norwegian, and Danish residents of the state, as we have seen, were not nearly as unanimous in their stand as their German brethren. In 1890, in fact, a large number of them continued to support Hoard. Even in those counties where the Germans and Scandinavians were nearly equal in population, the latter seem to have lessened the effect of the German wrath against the governor.

For example, Door, Jackson, Juneau, Rock, and Trempeleau counties with such a mixture of population supported Hoard in 1890, although admittedly by smaller margins than previously. The same was true of Waupaca, where the two important Danish centers, Farmington and Lind, gave him a sizeable plurality. Nevertheless, despite such occasional tempering influences, in the final analysis the German vote proved decisive in a majority of counties, and the Democratic Party reaped the reward in the form of a landslide victory.

This victory did not still the fears of the Germans, however, regarding the future of their schools, language, and national traditions. From Milwaukee, the *Seebote* warned that the dangers of "revolutionary plotting" against them had not ceased with the election of Peck to the governorship. For example, the organization called "the Patriotic Sons of America" was spread throughout the country, and its members numbered in the thousands. Furthermore, the Republican Party had not yet renounced its belief in compulsory education in the English language as manifested in the Wisconsin law of 1889. "Therefore, attention, ye Germans!" said the *Seebote*. "Keep track of the doings of these arch-nativists. . . . If we want to keep our best and most precious possessions, we must not allow ourselves to be lulled asleep. Let us be on the watch, therefore. We owe it to ourselves and to our children."[248]

As for the Bennett Law itself, the Democratic platform had pledged to repeal the controversial statute, and the Party now hastened to fulfill its promise. O. E. Wells, who replaced Thayer as the new State Superintendent of Public Instruction, suggested this course of action in a report delivered before the State Teachers' Association on December 30, 1890. Compulsory school legislation of the type represented in the 1889 statute, he charged, was both unnecessary and inoperative, and should not be allowed to remain in force.[249] The actual initiation of repeal procedures, however, was the work of newly elected Governor George Peck in his annual Governor's message at the opening session of the Wisconsin State Legislature. Thus, on January 15, 1891, two years after a similar speech by Governor William D. Hoard had prompted the passage of the Bennett measure, Peck stated the case for its annulment. He said:

> Chapter 519 of the laws of 1889 has been the source of much discussion and dissension in our state. In my judgment

---

248   Translated from the *Seebote* in the *Milwaukee Sentinel*, November 17, 1890, p. 4.
249   *Wisconsin State Journal*, December 30, 1890, p. 4.

this act, so far as it refers to educational matters, is unwise and unnecessary. In many of its provisions it is an arbitrary and unjustifiable interference with parental rights, individual freedom and the liberty of conscience, and I therefore recommend its prompt repeal.[250]

The Legislature quickly responded to this recommendation. Indeed, the very first bill (No. 1, A) presented to the Assembly on January 20, 1891, by the Democratic representative Philip Schmitz, Jr., called for the repeal of the Bennett Law. On the same day, in the Senate, a similar bill was proposed by Herman Kroeger (Dem.) of Milwaukee, who ironically had both approved and voted for the measure in 1889.[251]

Actual passage of the repeal law was rapid, once introduced, but the badly outnumbered Republicans did not surrender entirely without a struggle. The very next evening, in fact, after the bill was introduced, Republican members of both houses of the legislature met in secret caucus in the court house with Henry C. Payne, the party campaign manager, acting as chairman. The result was agreement on a substitute measure that would include the principles of the old law endorsed by the party platform, but that would also remove any clause that could possibly be construed as an attack upon or interference with parochial schools.

Pertinent sections of the amended bill called for every parent or guardian of a child between the ages of 7 and 13 to send him to "some public or private or *parochial* school" [emphasis added] for at least 12 weeks of the year. Section 4, the new English language clause, provided that each child in the appropriate age group receive enough instruction in the English language to be able to

---

250 *Wisconsin Governor's Messages and Accompanying Documents*, I (Madison, 1891), 13-14.
251 *Assembly Journal*, 1891, p. 31; *Senate Journal*, 1891, p. 28.

read and write it, while at the same time it stipulated clearly that nothing in the act should be construed as an attempt "to prohibit the teaching of any other language or branches of learning." In this substitute bill, the "district clause" was also eliminated and the right of appeal to a jury trial guaranteed.

By thus voluntarily removing all former objections to the Bennett Law and offering the amended bill to the legislature, as was done the next day (January 22), the Republicans hoped to force the Democrats to clarify their stand on the basic principle of compulsory education. In the words of a member of the secret caucus, their object was to force their opponents to "fish, cut bait, or go ashore."[252]

This bill stood little chance of passing, however, and thus after its swift defeat, the Republicans were once more forced to try a new approach. In the Assembly, two Republican members of the Committee on Education presented a minority report against passage of Bill No. 1, A. They did not deny that the Bennett Law contained some objectionable features, but they insisted it also included several provisions of great value to the educational system of the state. With much gratifying success, it had attempted to provide an education for all children of Wisconsin and to put an end to child labor. As yet, however, no law had been proposed to take on these great tasks after the Bennett Law was repealed. Therefore, the Republican spokesmen now recommended amendments to Bill No. 1, A, which would eliminate any objectionable features of the 1889 compulsory education act, while still maintaining its most basic principles.[253] These amendments, it should be noted, were essentially those proposed in the defeated substitute bill.

---

252 *Wisconsin State Journal*, January 22, 1891, p. 1.
253 "Minority Report" presented by Assemblymen Daniel J. Bill and Henry B. Dike of the Committee on Education, on January 23, 1891, printed in *Assembly Journal*, 1891, pp. 59-62.

Nevertheless, in all attempts to halt outright repeal of the Bennett Law—by amendment or, in the end, even by the dilatory tactics of parliamentary debate—Republican minority leaders faced a losing battle. A motion for adoption of the dissenting report by the two Republicans on the education committee was defeated in open assembly by a *viva voce* vote, and the chairman of that committee then reported out the repeal bill favorably for approval by the lower house. In one last effort to salvage something from the original Bennett enactment, Assemblyman Charles Osborn offered an amendment substituting a compulsory education bill, originally introduced by Clinton Textor, a Democrat, which omitted any English language clause. By a party vote of 65 to 31, however, the Assembly refused to accept the amendment.

The inevitable could no longer be resisted. Bill No. 1, A was submitted for final consideration, and by a vote of 87 to 14, it passed the lower house.[254] A similar result occurred in the Senate where the verdict was 21 to 11 in favor of repeal.[255] On February 5, 1891, therefore, the Act repealing the Bennett Law, which subsequently became Chapter 4 of the Laws of 1891, was signed by newly elected Governor George Peck.[256]

As these legislative records indicate, not all Republicans had voted to retain the Bennett measure, and this fact stirred some resentment among die-hard party members who saw their behavior as an abandonment of principle and a resort to political opportunism. In discussing this question editorially, however, the Republican-allied *Wisconsin State Journal* denied such charges

---

254 *Assembly Journal*, 1891, pp. 73-79. See also, *Wisconsin State Journal*, January 27, 1891, p. 1.
255 *Senate Journal*, 1891, pp. 28, 33, 46-47, 77, 103 (passage).
256 Wisconsin, *The Laws of Wisconsin, 1891*, I (Madison, 1891), p. 3.

and declared that those party members who had voted in favor of repeal had still adequately fulfilled their election promises.

> The republican platform pledged the party not to the Bennett Law in its entirety, but to the principles of the law, which are compulsory education and the right of the child to obtain a knowledge of the English language sufficient to enable it to read and write the same. These principles were embodied in the Republican substituted education bill. In voting for that measure the Republicans placed themselves on record in accordance with their platform. In voting for the Textor bill the Republicans showed a willingness to abandon one-half the principles in the Bennett Law, and in the Republican platform, simply because it was the best thing in sight, and as a stroke of parliamentary legerdemain to put the Democracy on record.[257]

Although admittedly this was still a vexatious question involving some political hairsplitting, the majority of Republicans in the Assembly who voted for repeal of the Bennett Law did so with the understanding that they would be given an opportunity to vote for a compulsory education bill containing at least some of the principles of the Textor amendments. Thus, they believed they had done their duty. The principle object for Republicans had never been to retain a defective law, albeit with some valuable provisions, when it was so clearly obnoxious to large segments of the population. Yet, in their eyes, the record would show that they had consistently done everything in their power to secure a satisfactory compulsory education law for the State of Wisconsin, and they would continue to do so in the future. Two months later, on April 17, 1891, such an act—simply stated without reference to an English language requirement—was signed into law. (See Appendix, Chapter 187 of *The Laws of 1891*.) [258]

---

257 *Wisconsin State Journal*, January 28, 1891, p. 2; January 30, p. 2.
258 *The Laws of Wisconsin, 1891*, I, 217-219. See Appendix, Chapter 187 of *The Laws of 1891*.

Bennett Law Debate as It Relates to U.S. Church-State Relations

Thus, as quickly as it had passed onto the statute books, the Bennett Law vanished from the political scene. A new law, with the simple provision that all children between the ages of seven and thirteen receive at least twelve weeks of instruction each year, replaced it. Nevertheless, in its brief history the Bennett measure illuminated fundamental issues involving the rights and duties of church and state in relation to one another, the future of public education in America, and the difficult process of nationalization faced by all new immigrant groups.

In addition, the question arises of just why the debate should have occurred when it did. There had been, after all, a compulsory education law on the books before the Bennett Act was even conceived, although admittedly it had become pretty much a dead letter. Nevertheless, why should the new law arouse such total abhorrence and antagonism among certain groups, while at the same time appear to many others as a beneficent and wholly necessary piece of legislation?

The answer cannot be found, I believe, in looking upon the Bennett Law simply as the focal point for an ordinary church-state controversy. Unlike a later Oregon law and other enactments of a similar nature, there was a second factor involved beyond the mere dislike of state interference with private school curricula. This additional element, which complicated the original issue and greatly increased the depth of the controversy, was quite clearly the English language provision of the Act. One is reminded again of the *Manitowoc County Chronicle*'s observation that if the two words "in English" were stricken from the law, not a churchman in the state would be found to oppose it.

The numerous critical comments of Bennett Law opponents provide ample verification of the need on the part of many immigrant groups to resist the encroachments of Americanization. Thus, the English language, far from being considered a method of advancement in the New World, was rather viewed as an unwelcome intrusion into their homes, churches, and schools. As knowledge of it spread among young people, many of them lost the willingness to communicate with their parents or grandparents in the language of their home country. Moreover, with the loss of the native tongue went allegiance to traditional customs and beliefs. Church membership declined where only the immigrant speech was used, and even parental authority over the young was subjected to perceptible erosion.

The testimony of early leaders of the English Evangelical Lutheran Church has already provided an indication of the belief cherished by many immigrant groups that loss of their native speech meant a corresponding loss of religious conviction. Little wonder then that these nationality groups should resist any attempt, real or imagined, to further loosen their hold on the traditions and values that they held most dear. Beware, the cry went forth. The true aim of the law is not to educate your children, but rather to tear from you the beloved native speech and precious heritage brought with you from the fatherland.

Nevertheless, if the Bennett Law with its English-language clause provided a convenient focal point for all the vague fears of immigrant groups concerning the problem of accommodating themselves and their institutions to the New World society, other factors also combined to make the years 1889-1890 propitious for the eruption of such a controversy. First, the Germans had by this time become a political force to be reckoned with. In many cities and counties they formed the majority of the population. About 54 percent of the residents of Milwaukee, the largest, most cosmopolitan city in the state, had some German ancestry. Indeed, in the state as a whole, Germans composed the largest single immigrant group.

Nor were numbers alone their greatest strength. Generally, members of this nationality had settled in Wisconsin in highly compact groups under the strong leadership of articulate, well-educated priests and ministers. During the Bennett Law controversy, the pulpit served as a highly effective instrument for molding public opinion, while for those who could read, German-language newspapers such as the *Germania*, *Seebote*, *Excelsior*, and *Columbia* brought news of the law, as well as arguments against it. Finally, there was the fact that this large, organized, and ably led group possessed the means to resist any enactment of which they disapproved. Because of Wisconsin's very liberal citizenship and suffrage requirements, *any resident of one year who had declared his intention of becoming an American citizen was entitled to vote in* *state elections.*²⁵⁹ As the 1890 political contest proved, the Germans were indeed a force to be considered with respect by those who had offended them.

Yet, still another factor was at work creating the proper atmosphere for the Bennett Law controversy. This factor was one of time. To begin with, of course, the waves of immigrants who had found homes in Wisconsin since the 1840s had by now carved out their homesteads and successfully coped with the initial problems of building houses, clearing lands, and setting up communities.²⁶⁰ Thus, when the Bennett Law issue arose, they had time to ponder the questions involved, listen to opposing arguments, and actively campaign for the law's repeal.

More important than this, however, was the fact that a second generation had begun to grow up and with them a developing concern lest these children eventually eschew their European heritage for an American one derived from the country in which they grew to adulthood. Had the Bennett Law been passed in a later decade when increasing natural contact with English-speaking natives had already enabled these children to learn English as a matter of course, there would have been no need at all for the English provision of the Act. Rasmus B. Anderson had realized this, of course, when he warned the governor in his speech before the anti-Bennett Law convention that this totally unnecessary law would only stir up dangerous antagonism and bitterness among foreign groups at a time when the primacy of the English language in America was already guaranteed. Far better was it then, to allow

---

259 *Wisconsin Blue Book, 1891*, p. 369.
260 The largest German immigration into Wisconsin took place in the decades 1840 to 1850, 1850 to 1860, and 1880 to 1890. More specifically, the majority of this group arrived during the years 1846-1854 and 1881-1884. See Kate Everest Levi, "Geographical Origins," p. 302.

time and the natural course of events to remove the need for such a measure.

But Anderson's words went unheeded, and in the maelstrom of political-religious controversy that subsequently arose, Governor Hoard (and the Republican Party) paid the price for having tried to enforce and accelerate the gradual process of nationalization among a people who were determined to protect, for their children's sake, their language, their customs, and their religious heritage at whatever cost to themselves or others.

Nevertheless, although the governor met defeat for his stand in favor of the Bennett Law, the principles of that measure were not lost. Not only did the largely inevitable course of Americanization continue, but religious opponents of the law, anxious to show it had been unnecessary, began to implement its basic provisions in their own schools. Thus, the Lutheran historian, August Stellhorn, points out that practically every synod, whether Scandinavian, German, or English, took a new look at its school system and thereupon acted to improve teacher training, effect better supervision of their educational institutions, promote more satisfactory relations between the state and public schools, and generally to raise the academic standards of their own parochial school systems.[261]

In keeping with this program, it was announced on April 22, 1891, that the Lutherans had voluntarily revised their curriculum to include more English. By August, the *Manitowoc Pilot* reported that the parochial schools of Manitowoc County had improved their English instruction to such an extent that very few of them would have been disqualified under the Bennett Law.[262] Gradually,

---
261 Stellhorn, p. 247.
262 See Kellogg, "The Bennett Law," p. 24.

the curriculum in denominational schools began to parallel that of public schools, and English replaced German as the medium of instruction. By 1921, these religious institutions were conducting classes in English as many days during the year as public schools. Moreover, as a result of the continuing improvement of standards, many of them received full accreditation from the state.[263]

In short, spurred on by the new interest concerning education that had been one result of the Bennett Law debates, church leaders in subsequent years quite voluntarily proceeded to bring the academic requirements of their schools up to a level commensurate with those of public institutions, and even to adopt for use in classrooms the English language, so bitterly resisted by the original immigrants.

In addition, the partial beginning made by the Bennett Law in checking the worst abuses of child labor was not lost. The system for regulating the work of young children through the issuance of court permits, initiated by the school law of 1889, was retained even after its subsequent repeal two years later. Not until 1899 was the next serious attempt made to control the child labor problem in the state, when a minimum age of fourteen for all laborers was set, along with maximum working hours for children up to the age of sixteen. From 1911 onwards, these provisions were gradually strengthened, although the lack of compliance in rural areas continued to be a problem.

Similarly, with regard to compulsory education, the laws that followed the Bennett measure in 1901, 1903, 1907, 1921, and later years were generally not unlike the earlier controversial enactment in their requirements of attendance. Only the English language provision was eliminated. Also reflecting a concern for

---
263   Hattstaedt, pp. 77-78.

the earlier difficulties that had arisen among proponents and opponents of the Bennett Law, representatives of the state's parochial schools were invited to participate when the drafting of a new and more stringent law was undertaken in 1907. Thus, despite its rapid disappearance from the statute books, the influence of the 1889 compulsory education act continued to be felt in those two areas of difficulty it was originally designed to remedy.[264]

Politically, however, after the Republican debacle of 1890, the Bennett Law itself became a dead issue. The Republican City Convention of Milwaukee, meeting on February 17, 1892, declared that the measure had been "unwarranted by existing conditions, and unwise from any standpoint it may be viewed." Even more specifically, the party's state convention clearly stated that all debate on the subject was at an end.

> We regard the education issue of 1890 as permanently settled in this state, not to be renewed in any of its phases by the Republican Party or under its auspices; and this being true, we deprecate and denounce, upon considerations higher than party, as harmful in tendency, any further agitation on the subject, or any attempt by any one, or by any party, for any purpose, to create or foster division among our people by reason of it upon lines of religion, education, or nativity.[265]

In 1892, George Peck was once more victorious in the gubernatorial contest over the Republican candidate, former Senator John C. Spooner, but two years later a Republican resurgence enabled William B. Upham to capture that office by

---

264   William F. Raney, *Wisconsin, A Story of Progress* (New York, 1940), p. 389. Conrad E. Patzer, *Public Education in Wisconsin* (Madison, 1924), p. 77.
265   Quoted in Thomson, p. 239.

an astounding margin of 53,000 votes. To puzzled politicians, ex-Governor Hoard stated that the source of this great plurality was undoubtedly the young German Lutherans who had broken with the Democrats as a result of their dislike for the earlier party stand on compulsory education. Indeed, he said that he had received word from 408 such young German Lutheran Democrats in Jefferson County that this was the main reason they now planned to vote for the Republican ticket. If this were true in one county, Hoard speculated, it was undoubtedly true in the rest of the state.[266]

In actual fact, some church leaders did eventually come to regret their actions during the Bennett Law crisis and to look upon the governor's role in it with more tolerance. In 1910, for example, Hoard was urged by many German Lutherans in his district to run for Congress so that they could provide him with practical evidence of their changed attitude. A delegation that visited him at his home stated:

> We, as Lutherans, voted against you in 1890, and under most serious misapprehension. Ever since that time we have felt that we did you a great wrong, and we have longed for some opportunity whereby we could record a vote for you for some important position of leadership, or again as a candidate for governor, or as a member of Congress, and we assure you that if you will accept such a candidacy that you will receive the united support of the German Lutheran people in this district.

In addition, the Lutheran Synod meeting in Fort Atkinson dispatched a delegation of clergymen to Hoard's home to express regret that they had misunderstood his intentions and the meaning of the law he championed. Should a similar question arise, they

---

266 Letter to Rasmus B. Anderson, in Hoard's *Personal Papers*, p. 2. See also Appendix to Anderson's *Life Story*, p. 675.

assured him, the Lutheran Church in Wisconsin would be solidly in favor of it.[267]

In general then, although the Bennett Law was effectively buried by the election results of 1890, its effect was more real and far-reaching than its utter defeat at the polls would apparently warrant. Never again, despite a brief flare-up of anti-German feeling during World War I, was the right of a church to regulate its own parochial schools challenged by the state. More important, however, was the fact that with each passing year the problems of nationalization diminished. The question that loomed so large in the minds of early immigrants, the seeming threat to their churches and schools posed by the Bennett Law with its irritating insistence on knowledge of the English language, was of little consequence to third generation Americans. To these men and women, English—not German—was their native tongue, and memories of a European homeland did not exist. Indeed, by 1925, there would not only have been little resistance to a Bennett Law, but there would have been no need for one.

Clearly, then, the furor that surrounded passage of the ill-fated compulsory-education law denoted more than a mere test case in the ever-evolving balance of church-state relationships in the United States. In looking back upon this short period of Wisconsin's history, the contemporary scholar must never lose sight of the fact that it served to mark as well one more milestone in the slow, arduous, and often painful process by which both immigrant peoples and immigrant institutions were transformed into that vague and complex state know as "American."

---

267 Quoted in Rankin, p. 136.

Appendix I

From *The Laws of Wisconsin, 1889*, pp. 729-733.
Bill No. 841, A.   Published April 27, 1889.

Chapter 519

An Act concerning the education and employment of children.

The people of the state of Wisconsin, represented in senate and assembly do enact as follows:

Section 1. Every parent or other person having under his control a child between the ages of seven and fourteen years, shall annually cause such child to attend some public or private day school in the city, town or district in which he resides, for a period not less than twelve weeks each year, which number of weeks shall be fixed prior to the first day of September in each year, by the board of education or board of direction of the city, town or district, and for a portion or portions thereof, to be so fixed by such boards, the attendance shall be consecutive, and such boards shall, at least ten days prior to the beginning of such period, publish the time or times of attendance, in such manner as such boards shall direct; provided that such boards shall not fix such compulsory period at more than twenty-four weeks in each year.

Section 2. For every neglect of such duty the person having such control and so offending shall forfeit to the use of the public schools of such city, town, or district a sum not less than three dollars ($3.00) nor more than twenty dollars ($20.00); and failure for each week or portion of a week on the part of any such person to comply with the provisions of this act, shall constitute a distinct offense; provided, that any such child shall be excused from attendance at school required by this act, by the board of education or school directors of the city, town or district in which such child resides upon its being shown to their satisfaction that the person so neglecting is not able to send such child to school, or that instruction has otherwise been given for a like period of time to such child in the elementary branches commonly taught in the public schools, or that such child has already acquired such elementary branches of learning, or that his physical or mental condition is such as to render attendance inexpedient or impracticable, and in all cases where such child shall be so excused the penalty herein provided shall not be incurred.

Section 3. Any person having control of a child who, with intent to evade the provisions of this act, shall make a willful false statement concerning the age of such child or the time such child has attended school, shall for such offense, forfeit a sum of not less than three dollars ($3) nor more than twenty dollars ($20) for the use of the public schools of such city, town or district.

Section 4. Five days prior to the beginning of any prosecution under this act such board shall cause a written notice to be personally served upon such person having control of any such child, with the provisions hereof, and if, upon the hearing of such prosecution, it shall appear to the satisfaction of the court that before or after the receipt of such notice such person has caused such child to attend a school as provided in this act in good faith and with intend (sic.) to continue such attendance, then the penalty provided by this act shall not be incurred.

Section 5. No school shall be regarded as a school, under this act, unless there shall be taught therein, as part of the elementary education of children, reading, writing, arithmetic, and United States history, ***in the English language*** [emphasis added].

Section 6. Prosecution under this Act shall only be instituted and carried on by the authority of such boards, and shall be brought in the name of said boards, and all fines and penalties, when collected, shall be paid to the school treasurer of such city, town or district, or other officer entitled to receive school moneys, the same to be held and accounted for as other school moneys received for school purposes.

Section 7. Jurisdiction to enforce the penalties herein described in this act is hereby conferred on justices of the peace and police magistrates within their respective counties.

Section 8. Any child between the ages of nine and fourteen years, who, without leave and against the will of his parent, guardian or other person having the right to control such child, habitually absents himself from the school to which he is sent or directed to be sent, and is beyond the control of his parent or guardian or other person having the right to control such child in that regard, and wanders or loiters in streets, alleys or other public places, shall be deemed a truant child, and on such truancy being alleged and proved, such truant child shall be adjudged a dependent child in like manner as is now provided by law for the adjudication of dependent children, and on being so adjudged dependent may be committed in like manner for such time not exceeding two years, as the judge or court having the jurisdiction of the matter may determine.

Any child so committed may, upon proof of amendment, or for other sufficient cause shown upon a hearing of the case be discharged by such judge or court at any time, but such child shall not be so confined after the age of fourteen years, nor shall he be bound or apprenticed nor placed out of any school to which he shall be committed.

Officers appointed by the board of education or board of school directors shall have power and authority to take a truant child found on the streets, alleys or other public places during school hours to such school conveniently located to the home of such child, as may be designated and requested by such parent, guardian or other person having the right to control such child, and such officer shall ascertain from such parent, guardian or other person having the right to control such child; or in the case such child has no parent, guardian or other person in control, then to the public school situated in the district where such child lives, or to such public school as such board may direct.

Section 9. No child under thirteen years of age shall be employed or allowed to work by any person, company, firm or corporation at labor or service in any shop, factory, mine, store, place of manufacture, business or amusement except as hereinafter provided.

Section 10. The judge of the county court in the county where the child resides and is to be employed or to work may by order of record, grant a permit to any child over ten years to be exempt and in such county from the operation of this act as to such employment, and to such extent, and for such time and on such terms as may be named in such permit, on its being shown to his satisfaction that such child can read and write the English language and that it is fit and proper considering the lack of means of support of the family of which such child is a member that such permit should be granted, and such permit may be rescinded by any such judge on written notice to such child, or to any person having control of or employing such child. Such permit must state the age, place of residence and the amount of school attendance prior to the granting of such permit with a record of such permits to be kept in such court.

The court may, when the business of the court requires, appoint a suitable person to hear and report on all applications for the issuance and rescission of permits, and may on hearing such report grant or refuse such application. Such person is to be paid a reasonable compensation by the county, to be fixed by the county board. Such person shall be an officer of the court, and removable by an order of court at any time. No charge or fee shall be required in any matter under this section.

Section 11. No child shall be so employed or work who does not present such permit and every person before employing or permitting such child to so labor, or be at service shall require and retain such permit, and shall keep the same together with a correct list of all children so employed posted in a conspicuous manner in the place of employment, and shall show such list on demand, to any school officer or teacher or police officer.

Section 12. Any person, company, or corporation who employs or permits to be employed or to work any child in violation of this act and any person having the control of any such child who permits such employment or work, shall for every offense forfeit a sum of not less than ten dollars ($10), nor more than fifty dollars ($50), for the use of the public school of such city, town or district, and every day of such illegal employment shall constitute a distinct offense.

Section 13. Any person having control of or in his employ a child who, with intent to evade the provisions of this act, shall make a false statement concerning the age of such child or the time such child has attended school or shall instruct such child to make any false statement, shall, for such offense forfeit a sum of not less than ten dollars ($10) nor more than fifty dollars ($50), for the use of the public schools of such city, town or district.

Section 14. This act shall take effect and be in force from and after its passage and publication.

Approved April 18, 1889.

Appendix II

From *The Laws of Wisconsin, 1891*, pp. 217-219.
Bill No. 449, A.   Published April 17, 1891.

Chapter 187

An Act to promote school attendance and restrain truancy.

The people of the state of Wisconsin, represented in senate and assembly, do enact as follows:

Section 1.   Every parent or other person having under his control any child between the ages of seven and thirteen years shall cause such child to attend, for at least twelve weeks in each and every school year, some public or private school; provided, however, that this act shall not apply to any child that has been or is being otherwise instructed, for a like period of time in the elementary branches of learning, or that has already acquired such knowledge, or whose mental or physical condition is such as to render his or her attendance at school and application to study inexpedient or impracticable, or who lives more than two miles from any school by the nearest traveled road, or who is excused for sufficient reasons by any court of record. Every person who shall violate the provisions of this section, shall upon conviction thereof, be fined in any sum not less than three dollars nor more than twenty dollars for each and every offense.

Section 2. It shall be the duty of the director of any school district, or the president of the board of education of any incorporated village or city, or any truant officers appointed by such board of education, to prosecute any offense occurring under this act, and such person neglecting to prosecute for such fine within fifteen days after a written notice has been served upon him, by any qualified elector or tax-payer within the district, village or city within which the offending party shall reside, shall be liable to a fine of not less than ten nor more than twenty dollars for each and every offense.

Section 3. The board of education of every city and incorporated village, and the district school board in every school district, may appoint one or more persons, who shall be designated as truant officers, whose duty it shall be, acting discreetly, to apprehend upon view, all children between seven and thirteen years of age, who habitually frequent and loiter about public places, and have no lawful occupation, and place such children, when so apprehended, in such schools as the parent or other person having control of such children may designate; and such officers shall report all cases of truancy to their respective boards of education, within a reasonable time. The persons appointed such truant officers shall be entitled to such compensation as shall be fixed by the boards appointing them and such compensation may be paid out of the school fund.

Section 4. The fines provided for by this act shall, when collected, be paid over by the officers collecting the same to the proper school treasury of the city, village, or school district in which such person convicted resides, to be applied and accounted for by such treasurers in the same way as other moneys raised for school purposes, and shall be placed by such treasurers to the credit of any city or district in which such person resided at the time of conviction.

Section 5. It shall be the duty of all officers empowered to take the annual school census to ascertain the number of children between the ages of seven and thirteen years, in their respective districts, the number of children between such ages who do not attend school and, in so far as possible, the cause or causes of such failure to attend school.

Section 6. All acts or portions of acts inconsistent with this act are hereby repealed.

Section 7. This act shall take effect and be in force from and after its passage and publication.

Approved April 6, 1891.

Bibliographical Note

Secondary Sources

Among the relatively few articles published on the Bennett Law controversy, the best is that of Louise Phelps Kellogg, "The Bennett Law in Wisconsin," *Wisconsin Magazine of History*, II (September, 1918), 3-25. Writing during the First World War, Dr. Kellogg was acutely aware of the problems of acculturation faced by the state's German population and saw in the current turmoil a reflection of the earlier Bennett Law agitation. Her article, therefore, is concerned primarily with the social significance of the educational controversy for German-Americans.

In it she provides some very valuable insight into the whole question of "Americanization," although generally her point of view is limited to this particular nationality group. No attempt is made, for example, to examine the related problems of accommodation to the New World faced by immigrant churches in this period. In addition, the whole question of Cahenslyism is ignored, and the wide divisions between Irish and German Catholics, as well as Scandinavian and German Lutherans, in such matters are scarcely mentioned. In short, while Dr. Kellogg's article is thorough with regard to the specific German-American nationality group and her awareness of the relationship between acculturation and the Bennett Law debate is sound, in order to bring the entire question into focus further discussion of the religious manifestations of the Americanization problem is needed.

A second major article, which aims at a rebuttal of the Kellogg thesis, is that of William F. Whyte, "The Bennett Law Campaign in Wisconsin," *Wis. Mag. of Hist.*, X (1927), 364-390. Doctor Whyte, raised in Watertown, a predominantly German settlement, was despite his Republican background a staunch friend of many who opposed the Bennett Law. Because of his close association with the debate, in fact, his article comes near to being a source document itself. The burden of his argument is that the act was useless and that Hoard blundered inexcusably in inflicting it upon the state, thereby alienating many loyal immigrant-Americans and bringing his own party to disaster politically. In conjunction with this article, Joseph Schafer's "Editorial Comment" in the same issue of the *Wisconsin Magazine of History* (pp. 457-461) should be read. While generally agreeing that the Bennett Law was unwise, Schafer points out several other political factors ignored by Whyte in the heat of discussion and concludes that the compulsory education law was not solely responsible for the Republican defeat in 1890.

In addition to these two central articles, background material for this paper was obtained from a number of political and educational histories of the state. William F. Raney's *Wisconsin, A Story of Progress* (New York, 1940) was useful in examining the relationship of the Bennett Law to the development of child labor legislation in Wisconsin. Other works that touch briefly upon the controversy include Henry C. Campbell, ed., *Wisconsin in Three Centuries, 1643-1903* (New York, 1906), Ralph G. Plumb, *Badger Politics, 1836-1930* (Manitowoc, Wis., 1930), and Alexander M. Thomson, *A Political History of Wisconsin* (Milwaukee, 1900). Thomson's work was the most effective in pointing out the later changed attitude of the Republicans toward the Bennett Law in the elections of 1892 and 1894. Of the various histories of education in the state, John W. Stearns' *The Columbian History of Education in Wisconsin* (Milwaukee, 1893) generally proved less comprehensive than Conrad E. Patzer's *Public Education in Wisconsin* (Madison, 1924). The latter was useful for placing the Bennett Law in context with earlier and later compulsory education measures.

Wisconsin Historical Society publications contain numerous helpful studies of the various nationality groups that made up Wisconsin's population in the 19th century. A general survey of the topic is John G. Gregory, "Foreign Immigration to Wisconsin," in Wis. Hist. Soc. *Proceedings, 1901* (Madison, 1901), pp. 137-143. For the Germans, a sympathetic accounting of their political importance can be found in W. Hense-Jensen, "Influence of Germans in Wisconsin," Wis. Hist. Soc. *Proceedings, 1901*, pp. 144-147. The most valuable information, however, was obtained from Kate A. Everest, "How Wisconsin Came By Its Large German Element," Wis. Hist. Soc. *Collections*, XII (Madison, 1892), 299-334 and Kate Everest Levi, "Geographical Origins of German Immigration to Wisconsin," Wis. Hist. Soc. *Collections*, XIV (Madison, 1898), 341-393. With their author's thorough study of the reasons for the early immigration from Germany, regions from which these people originally came, and patterns of settlement when they reached Wisconsin, these two articles do much to dispel the generally held belief that the 1848 Revolution provided most of the state's German population. In addition, they provide valuable insight into the attitude of many immigrants toward a law that was viewed as a threat to the maintenance of their Old-World customs and traditions. Several useful demographic maps and statistical tables are included. William F. Whyte, "The Settlement of the Town of Lebanon, Dodge County," Wis. Hist. Soc. *Proceedings, 1915* (Madison, 1915), pp. 99-110, also touches briefly on this topic.

For a good discussion of the liberal "Forty-Eighters" and their reactions to acculturation, see Ernest Bruncken, "The Political Activity of Wisconsin Germans, 1854-1860," Wis. Hist. Soc. *Proceedings, 1901* (Madison, 1901), pp. 190-211. The most thorough treatment of the German immigrants' development in a specific locality is Bayrd Still's *Milwaukee, The History of a City* (Madison, 1965), while for a general analysis of the problems of another foreign group, the Irish Americans, Sister Justille McDonald's *History of the Irish in Wisconsin in the 19th Century* (Washington, 1954) proves valuable. Those wishing more information on the various nationality groups in the state will find the Wisconsin Historical Society's publication, *Subject Bibliography of Wisconsin History*, compiled by Leroy Schlinkert (Madison, 1947), a useful tool.

The standard work on the development of anti-foreign and anti-Catholic feeling in the 19th century is John Higham's *Strangers in the Land* (New Brunswick, N.J., 1955). This is a well-documented treatment of the continuing flux of such nativist movements throughout American history with one chapter devoted to the increasing outbursts in the late 1800's and the reasons for them. Humphrey J. Desmond, *The A.P.A. Movement, A Sketch* (Washington, 1912) is a more specific discussion of one such group that gained much strength in the Middle West at the time. A Catholic view of this movement and its relationship to compulsory education laws is presented in Thomas J. Jenkins, "A.P.A. Conspirators," *Catholic World*, LVII (1893), 685-693.

In gathering information on secular political leaders in the controversy, two biographies (both sympathetic to their subjects) were helpful. Dorothy Ganfield Fowler's *John Coit Spooner, Defender of Presidents* (New York, 1961) depicted the attitude of those Republicans who disagreed with the Wisconsin governor's stand on the Bennett Law issue, while in George W. Rankin's *William Dempster Hoard* (Fort Atkinson, 1925) early events in his life were revealed that may have influenced his decision to support compulsory education and a universal knowledge of the English language.

A number of sources were useful in the task of checking biographical facts and other data on prominent figures in the debate. They include: Andrew J. Aikens and Lewis A. Proctor, *Men of Progress, Wisconsin* (Milwaukee, 1897); John R. Berryman, *History of the Bench and Bar of Wisconsin*, I (Chicago, 1898); *The Biographical Dictionary and Portrait Gallery of Representative Men of Chicago, Wisconsin* (Chicago and New York, 1895); *Dictionary of Wisconsin Biography* (Madison, 1960); *Evening Wisconsin Newspaper Reference Book* (Milwaukee, 1914); *Report of the Annual Meeting of the Wisconsin State Bar Association of 1900* (Madison, 1901); *Soldiers' and Citizens' Album of Biographical Record*, II (Chicago, 1890); Ellis B. Usher, *Wisconsin, Its Story and Biography*, IV (Chicago and

New York, 1914); and Williams Publishing Company, *Notable Men of Wisconsin* (Milwaukee, 1902).

For a general survey of church-state relations in the United States, Anson Phelps Stokes and Leo Pfeffer, *Church and State in the United States* (New York, Evanston, and London, 1964) is a standard work. Although its reference to the Bennett Law is brief and it tends to further the inaccurate view that the prime motivation for its enactment was anti-foreign and anti-Catholic bias, its coverage of the broader topic of religious history in the United States is valuable. Two major works dealing with the problem of immigrant churches in America are Will Herberg, *Protestant–Catholic–Jew* (New York, Doubleday Anchor Paperback, 1960) and H. Richard Niebuhr, *The Social Sources of Denominationalism* (Cleveland and New York, Meridian Paperback, 1964). Both contain discussions of the divisions that occurred between nationality groups in the various denominations when the question of Americanization arose. Herberg's book is especially good in describing the friction that developed between Irish and German Catholics in the 19th century. Another work that examines the problems of German-American Catholics in this period is that of Colman James Barry, *The Catholic Church and German-Americans*, Catholic University of America *Studies*, XL (1953).

For a broad survey of Catholic history in the state, Harry H. Heming, *History of the Catholic Church in Wisconsin* (Milwaukee, 1896) is useful. The treatment of the Bennett Law controversy is openly unfriendly to Hoard, but important source documents such as the Bishops' Manifesto are quoted in full. Two biographies of value are John T. Ellis, *James Cardinal Gibbons* (Milwaukee, 1952) and Benjamin J. Blied, *Three Archbishops of Milwaukee* (Milwaukee, 1955). The latter contains a sympathetic discussion of Bishop Frederick X. Katzer, one of the chief opponents of the Bennett Law, and his role in that debate, as well as in the Cahensly movement. A less complimentary interpretation may be found in the work by John Ellis.

Aspects of Lutheran Church history in the state have been treated by August C. Stellhorn in his *Schools of the Lutheran Church—Missouri Synod* (St. Louis, 1963). Stellhorn examines both the Illinois and Wisconsin compulsory education statutes and concludes that they represented a clear-cut encroachment by the state on religious rights which was inspired by nativism. His allusion to the Bennett Law as a product of Boston's Committee of One Hundred, however, is erroneous. An earlier work—Otto F. Hattstaedt, *History of the Southern Wisconsin District of the Evangelical Lutheran Synod of Missouri, Ohio, and other States* (St. Louis, 1928), trans. in *Wis. Hist. Records Survey*, W.P.A., Madison, 1941, contains a similar bias, but the *Augustana Lutheran Church of America, 1860-1910: The Formative Period* (Davenport, Iowa, 1965) by Oscar Nils Olson reveals an awareness of the difficulties faced by many Germans and Scandinavians in accommodating themselves to the new land.

Finally, as a general overview of the 19th century and for certain specific facts, such as the outcome of the 1890 Congressional elections or importance of the McKinley tariff issue, the text by T. Harry Williams, Richard N. Current, and Frank Freidel, *A History of the United States [since 1865]* (New York, 1960) has been helpful.

Primary Sources

Primary sources dealing with both the law and the general period in political and church history are plentiful, and the State

Historical Society of Wisconsin at Madison contains a large collection of state publications, campaign pamphlets, newspapers, manuscripts, and other documents pertinent to the subject.

Official state publications of value include the "Biennial Report of the State Superintendent of the State of Wisconsin for the years 1887-1888," in *Wisconsin Governor's Message and Accompanying Documents (1887-1888)*, I (Madison, 1889) and the "Biennial Report of the State Superintendent of the State of Wisconsin for the Two Years Ending June 30, 1890," in *Wisconsin Governor's Message and Accompanying Documents, 1891*, I (Madison, 1891). State Superintendent Jesse B. Thayer's circular letter explaining the provisions and requirements of the Bennett Law—*From the Office of State Superintendent of Schools to Boards of Education, Boards of Directors, and School District Boards* (Madison, 1890)—is also available. Wisconsin *Blue Books* for the years 1887-1895 provided basic facts regarding population and election statistics, suffrage requirements, capsule biographies of legislators, and other useful information. Important speeches of both Governor Hoard and Governor Peck before the Legislature are printed in *Governors' Messages: Wisconsin, 1876-1899* (Madison, n.d.); *Wisconsin Governor's Message and Accompanying Documents, (1887-1888)*, I (Madison, 1889); and *Wisconsin Governor's Message and Accompanying Documents, 1891*, I (Madison, 1891). For a record of the Bennett Law's passage and repeal, see the Wisconsin Assembly and Senate *Journals* for the years 1889 and 1891.

Statistics on religious affiliation and national origin for the Wisconsin population were obtained from the *Report on the Population of the United States at the 11th Census: 1890. Part I: Population* (Washington, D.C., 1895) and the *U.S. Census Bulletins: "Statistics of Churches,"* No. 23, pp. 1-27; no. 101, pp.

1-42; no. 152, pp. 1-52 (Washington, D.C., 1891). A small unsigned pamphlet entitled *Catholic Statistics for Wisconsin, 1891* (n.p., 1891) in possession of the Wisconsin Historical Society, *Hoffman's Catholic Directory* (Milwaukee, 1889), and statistics of the German Evangelical Lutheran Church printed as an appendix to Christian Koerner's *The Bennett Law and the German Parochial Schools of Wisconsin* (Milwaukee, 1890) were also useful.

The attitude of smaller parties and pressure groups within the state regarding the compulsory education law and Bible-reading in the public schools is recorded in the Wisconsin W.C.T.U., *Minutes of the Seventeenth Annual Meeting of the Woman's Christian Temperance Union of Wisconsin, Held June 3, 4, 5, and 6, 1890* (Madison, 1890) and in the platforms of Prohibition and Union Labor parties published in the Wisconsin *Blue Book* for 1891.

A letter to the editor of *The Nation* (vol. 50, pp. 240-241), dated March 15, 1890, from Bradley G. Schley of Milwaukee, provides a well-balanced discussion of the measure by a contemporary observer. Schley briefly summarizes the major provisions of the statute, as well as arguments both for and against it.

In addition, the Wisconsin Historical Society has in its possession a collection of campaign pamphlets, broadsides, poems, and songs printed in English and several foreign languages, which were distributed during the Bennett Law controversy. For convenience many of them have been bound and are catalogued as *Bound Bennett Law Pamphlets*. Some of those most characteristic of the opposition's stand include: The Anti-Bennett State Central Committee, *Pamphlet No. 2. The Bennett Law* (n.p., n.d.); *A Baptist Opinion of the Bennett Law* (n.p., n.d.); *Declarations and Resolutions adopted by a meeting of representative laymen of the German protestant churches in Milwaukee, held*

Febr. 27ᵗʰ, (1890) . . . (Milwaukee, 1890); German Lutheran Committee on the Present School Law, *Objections to the Present Compulsory School Law of Illinois* (n.p., n.d.); *A Presbyterian Opinion on the Bennett Law* (n.p., n.d.). The following pamphlets represent arguments in favor of the education act: *The Bennett Law Analyzed* (n.p., n.d.); Democratic Bennett Law League, *Address of the Democratic Bennett Law League* (Milwaukee, 1890); and *The Duty of the State to Its Future Citizens—Read and Consider* (n.p., 1890). An unsigned pamphlet, *"The Little Red Schoolhouse." Does a Vote for the Republican Ticket Mean a Vote in Defense of the Common School?* (n.p., n.d.), appears to be the work of the Prohibition Party. Also included in this material are two clippings from the nativist publication *America*: Duane Mowry, "The Bennett School Law," *America*, January 30, 1890, and by the same author, "The Situation in Wisconsin," *America*, July 24, 1890.

Newspapers provided another major source of information on the controversy, and the author is indebted once again to the Wisconsin Historical Society, which owns an unusually fine collection of papers and journals. Available on microfilm or in bound volumes are virtually every daily, weekly, and semi-weekly paper published in the state for that period, including those printed in a foreign language. An extremely useful guide to the entire collection is Ada Tyng Griswold's *Annotated Catalogue of Newspaper Files in the Library of the State Historical Society of Wisconsin* (Madison, 1911). This catalogue provides for each paper or journal the names of succeeding editors, information on religious or political affiliation, and editorial policies, whether printed in a language other than English, and the number of issues preserved in the library.

Those newspapers used most frequently for this study include the Republican-oriented *Milwaukee Sentinel* and *Wisconsin State Journal*, along with two influential Democratic organs, *The Milwaukee Journal* and the *Madison Daily Democrat*. For additional insight into the reactions to the Bennett Law among the people of the neighboring state of Illinois, then undergoing its own debate on a similar measure, the *Chicago Tribune* (Rep. with Independent leanings) and the *Chicago Herald* (Dem.) prove helpful. Two German-language papers of value to researchers are the *Excelsior* (Catholic) and the *Germania* (Lutheran), both printed in Milwaukee. In addition, translations of articles from these and other German organs are often printed in the major English-language papers such as the *Milwaukee Sentinel*.

Two volumes of *Bennett Law Newspaper Clippings* preserved in the State Historical Society Library provide a general survey of the events of the campaign, as well as editorial comment, but the collection is not as useful as it might be, since the compiler on many occasions cut off the date of the article and even the name of the newspaper from which it came. For numerous excerpts from newspaper editorials discussing the law and its meaning for Church-State relations in America, which were published throughout the country, see "Compulsory English Education: The Bennett Law in Wisconsin," printed in *Public Opinion*, IX (April 12, 1890), 1-4.

Manuscript collections preserved in the Society Library are also extensive, including those of the following Republican political leaders: Nils P. Haugen, William D. Hoard, and Jeremiah M. Rusk. A useful index for these papers is the *Guide to the Manuscripts of the Wisconsin Historical Society*, edited by Alice E. Smith (Madison,

1944). Volumes 1-3 (1888-1889) of Haugen's *Letter Books* contain frequent allusions to the developing controversy. Similarly, the papers of Jermiah M. Rusk, volumes 6-11 (March 1889-September 1891) of his *Letters to Colonel Henry Casson*, provide a further understanding of the attitudes of those professional politicians who were anxious to preserve their party's hegemony in state and national affairs and, therefore, looked upon the Bennett Law as a political blunder.

The most extensive collection, however, is that of William D. Hoard. Several boxes of his *Personal Papers* are available containing various campaign speeches, pertinent clippings from his own paper (*Hoard's Dairyman*), and the original copy of a letter to Rasmus B. Anderson subsequently published in the latter's autobiography. In addition, seven volumes of *Private Letter Books* (volumes 15-21, January 1889-September 1892) provide insight into the governor's reaction to the law. This collection is indispensable for a true understanding of Hoard's motivation for championing the principles of the act, containing his letters to both critics and defenders, clergymen and laymen, as well as other politicians during the debate about the law.

In conjunction with these manuscript collections, the papers of Louise Phelps Kellogg contain several pertinent documents. The first of these is a typewritten copy of the "Notes of an Interview with ex-Governor *William Dempster Hoard*, at his home in Fort Atkinson, August 12 and 13, 1918." Many questions bearing on the Bennett Law controversy were discussed during the interview. Included in this collection also is Hoard's own account of a visit in the summer of 1890 by a group of Lutheran ministers who sought to persuade him to disclaim the Bennett

Law and a reprint of an article by William H. Hobbs, entitled "A Pioneer Movement for Americanization," published in *The Outlook*, April 24, 1918. The latter is a retrospective view of the Bennett Law controversy written at a time during World War I, when a wave of anti-German feeling was enveloping the country and particularly the Middle West.

Memoirs and publications by prominent party figures involved in the debate include: Rasmus B. Anderson, *Life Story of Rasmus B. Anderson, written by himself with the assistance of Albert O. Barton* (Madison, 1917); Nils P. Haugen, *Pioneer and Political Reminiscences* (Evansville, Wis., 1929); and John C. Spooner, *Senator John C. Spooner on Compulsory Education* (Milwaukee, 1890) in *Bound Bennett Law Pamphlets*. For the Democrats, party leader William F. Vilas outlined a defense of the opposition's stand and the grounds on which the law was found untenable in "'The Bennett Law' in Wisconsin," *Forum*, XII (October, 1891), 196-207.

The compulsory school law also caused some repercussions in the educational field. John Bascom, President of the University of Wisconsin from 1874 to 1886, in his article "A New Policy for the Public Schools," *Forum*, XI (March, 1891), 59-66, used the Bennett Law turmoil as one reason for advocating a joint system of public and parochial schools, both supported by public funds. E. M. Winston's rebuttal appears in "The School Controversy in Illinois," *Forum*, XII (October, 1891), 208-214, along with a discussion of the principles involved in such laws.

The Catholic position on the utilization of public funds for private schools and the relation of parochial schools to the state educational system was an important factor in the Wisconsin debates, especially in the eyes of many Protestant groups. The following articles by Catholic spokesmen reveal their concern over this important school question: Brother Azarias, "Religion in Education," *American Catholic Quarterly Review*, XVI (1891), 760-778; Brother Barbas, "Professor Fisher on 'Unsectarianism' in the Common Schools," *Am. Cath. Quart. Rev.*, XVII (1892), 176-190; Francis J. Chatard, "Are Catholics Right?," *Am. Cath. Quart. Rev.*, XV (1890), 560-575; Michael Hennessy, "Why Education Should Be Free," *Am. Cath. Quart. Rev.*, XVI (1891), 806-817; E.A. Higgins, "The American State and the Private School," *Catholic World*, LIII (July, 1891), 521-527; and John Murphy, "The Idea of a Parochial School," *Am. Cath. Quart. Rev.*, XVI (1891), 449-461.

Archbishop John Ireland of St. Paul also discussed the school question in an important speech in June 1890 before the National Education Association in which he advocated the adoption of a compromise plan for the support of public and parochial schools. For this address, as well as expressions of his sympathetic view toward the rapid Americanization of immigrant Catholics, see his book, *The Church and Modern Society* (Chicago and New York, 1896). A subsequent letter written to Cardinal Gibbons in defense of his speech to the N.E.A. against the attacks of Father Abbelen, Bishop Katzer, and other German-American Catholics is reprinted in John T. Ellis, ed., *Documents of American Catholic History* (Milwaukee, 1962). Also included in this collection are the Cahensly Memorial of 1891 and the Secret Oath of the American Protective Association (A.P.A.). A Catholic opinion opposed to the development of a distinctly American Catholic Church is presented in Thomas S. Preston's "American Catholicity," *Am. Cath. Quart. Rev.*, XVI (1891), 396-408.

Concerning the Lutheran Church and its own problems with Americanization in this period, the Reverend G. H. Gerberding's "Reminiscent Pioneering and Moralizing" in *Historical and Reminiscent Sketches: English Evangelical Lutheran Synod of the Northwest, 1891-1916* (n.p., 1916), 36-49, provides some informative and often amusing anecdotes on the resistance of many immigrants to the use of English in their churches.

Suggestions for Further Research

The possibilities for further research on the question of the effects of Americanization on religious opposition to compulsory educational laws during the 19th century seem promising. It would appear, at least in the state of Wisconsin, that the prevailing view of many of these school law controversies as a simple manifestation of church-state conflict must be broadened to include the emotional effects of acculturation on the immigrant churches in their resistance to such measures. How true this was in other parts of the country, however, remains to be studied.

The Edwards Act in Illinois (1889), which inspired a controversy not unlike that which occurred in Wisconsin is one obvious case for consideration. Although the Republican Party in power proved less intractable before church demands than Hoard and his supporters in the neighboring state, a similar fate awaited them at the polls in 1890. It would be interesting, therefore, to compare the progress of the debates in these two states, so much alike in population, economy, and political background, to determine how similar were the arguments of religious opponents of the law, whether the same divisions along nationality lines occurred, and what effects the more conciliatory attitude of Illinois Republicans had on the question. Whether the issues of Cahenslyism or Americanization appeared during the debates and, if so, how strong these issues became should also be a central consideration. Moreover, the resources for such a study would undoubtedly be extensive. Public documents, church records, newspapers, pamphlets, manuscript collections, and state educational and political histories should be as readily available as similar material in Wisconsin.

Additional possibilities for research include a study of one of the other states that passed a compulsory education law at this time, e.g., Ohio, New York, Massachusetts, or a comparison of any two or more of these states. The problem of Americanization is an interesting one, and its effects on political, social, and religious history provide ample opportunity for further investigation.

Bibliography

Public Documents

U.S. Bureau of the Census. *Report on the Population of the United States at the Eleventh Census: 1890. Part I: Population.* Washington, D.C., 1895.

U.S. Bureau of the Census. *U.S. Census Bulletins: "Statistics of Churches."* No. 23, pp. 1-27; No. 101, pp. 1-42; No. 152, pp. 1-52. Washington, D.C., 1891.

Wisconsin. Department of Public Instruction. "Biennial Report of the State Superintendent of the State of Wisconsin for the Years 1887-1888," in *Wisconsin: Governor's Message and Accompanying Documents, 1887-88.* Vol. 1. Madison, 1889.

Wisconsin. Department of Public Instruction. "Biennial Report of the State Superintendent of the State of Wisconsin for the Two Years Ending June 30, 1890," in Wisconsin, *Governor's Message and Accompanying Documents, 1891.* Vol. 1. Madison, 1891.

Wisconsin. *Governors' Messages: Wisconsin, 1876-1899.* Madison, n.d.

Wisconsin. *The Laws of Wisconsin, 1879.* Vol. 1. Madison, 1879.

Wisconsin. *The Laws of Wisconsin, 1889.* Vol. 1. Madison, 1889.

Wisconsin. *The Laws of Wisconsin, 1891.* Vol. 1. Madison, 1891.

Wisconsin. Secretary of State. *The Blue Book of the State of Wisconsin.* Milwaukee, 1887, 1889, 1891, 1893, 1895.

Wisconsin. *State of Wisconsin Assembly Journal.* Madison, 1889, 1891.

Wisconsin. *State of Wisconsin Senate Journal.* Madison, 1889, 1891.

Wisconsin. *Wisconsin Governor's Message and Accompanying Documents (1887-1888).* Vol. 1. Madison, 1889.

Wisconsin. *Wisconsin Governor's Message and Accompanying Documents, 1891.* Vol. 1. Madison, 1891.

Manuscripts

Haugen, Nils P. *Letter Books.* Vols. 1-3 (1889-1891).

Hoard, William Dempster. "Account of an Incident in which a group of Lutheran ministers visited Hoard in his office to speak out against the Bennett Law (summer of 1890)." (Written by Governor Hoard from memory and given to Louise Phelps Kellogg during an interview at his home in Fort Atkinson, August 12-13, 1918.) In *Kellogg Papers* at the Wisconsin Historical Society, Madison.

———. "Letter to Rasmus B. Anderson, December 23, 1915." Original copy in *Hoard's Personal Papers*, Wis. Hist. Soc. Also reprinted in Anderson, *Life Story*, Appendix, pp. 672-675.

———. *Personal Papers.* (Miscellaneous MSS in possession of Wis. Hist. Soc. dealing with political affairs in the State of Wisconsin, 1889-1892.)

———. *Private Letter Books of William Dempster Hoard.* Vols. 15-21. (January 1889 – September 1892).

Kellogg, Louise Phelps. "Notes of an Interview with Ex-Governor *William Dempster Hoard*," at his home at Fort Atkinson, August 12 and 13, 1918." (Typewritten, unpublished.) In *Kellogg Papers*, Wis. Hist. Soc.

Rusk, Jeremiah M. *Letter Books: Letters of Jeremiah M. Rusk to Colonel Henry Casson.* Vols. 6-11 (March 1889 – September 1891). In *Rusk Papers*, Wis. Hist. Soc.

Pamphlets and Newspapers

The Anti-Bennett State Central Committee. *Pamphlet No. 2. The Bennett Law.* N.p., n.d. In *Bound Bennett Law Pamphlets.* 8 pp.

A Baptist Opinion on the Bennett Law. N.p., n.d. In *Bound Bennett Law Pamphlets.* 2 pp.

The Bennett Law Analyzed. N.p., n.d. (Printed in English, German, Polish, Bohemian.) In *Bound Bennett Law Pamphlets.* 8 pp.

Bennett Law Newspaper Clippings. 2 Vols.

Bound Bennett Law Pamphlets. (*Collections* of broadsides, pamphlets, etc. printed in German, French, Polish, Bohemian, and English. Includes miscellaneous materials not elsewhere cited.)

Catholic Statistics for Wisconsin, 1891. N.p., 1891. 4 pp.

Chicago Tribune. April, 1890.

Declarations and Resolutions adopted by a meeting of representative laymen of the German protestant churches in Milwaukee, held Febr. 27th (1890).... Milwaukee, 1890. In *Bound Bennett Law Pamphlets.* 2 pp.

Democratic Bennett Law League. *Address of the Democratic Bennett Law League.* Milwaukee, 1890. 10 pp.

The Duty of the State to Its Future Citizens—Read and Consider. N.p., 1890. In *Bound Bennett Law Pamphlets.* 15 pp.

Excelsior. February, 1890.

German Lutheran Committee on the Present School Law. *Objections to the Present Compulsory School Law of Illinois.* N.p., n.d. In *Bound Bennett Law Pamphlets.* 30 pp.

"*The Little Red Schoolhouse.*" *Does a Vote for the Republican Party Mean a Vote In Defense of the Common Schools?* N.p., n.d. In *Bound Bennett Law Pamphlets.* 4 pp.

Koerner, Christian. *The Bennett Law and the German Parochial Schools of Wisconsin.* Milwaukee, 1890. *In Bound Bennett Law Pamphlets.* 32 pp.

Madison Daily Democrat. January 1889–March 1891.

Milwaukee Journal. January 1889–March 1891.

Milwaukee Sentinel. January 1889–March 1892.

Mowry, Duane. "The Bennett School Law," *America*, January 30, 1890. In *Bound Bennett Law Pamphlets.*

———. "The Situation in Wisconsin," *America*, July 24, 1890. In *Bound Bennett Law Pamphlets.*

A Presbyterian Opinion on the Bennett Law. N.p., n.d. In *Bound Bennett Law Pamphlets.*

Spooner, John C. *Senator Spooner on Compulsory Education.* (From his speech at the West Side Turner Hall, Milwaukee, Friday, October 3, 1890.) In *Bound Bennett Law Pamphlets.* 8 pp.

Thayer, J. B. *From the Office of the State Superintendent of Schools to Boards of Education, Boards of School Directors, and School District Boards.* Madison, 1890. In *Bound Bennett Law Pamphlets.* 4 pp.

The Underlying Principles of the Bennett Law. N.p., n.d. In *Bound Bennett Law Pamphlets.* 4 pp.

Wisconsin State Journal. January 1889–March 1891.

Books and Reports

Aikens, Andrew J. and Proctor, Lewis A., ed.'s. *Men of Progress, Wisconsin.* Milwaukee, 1897.

Anderson, Rasmus B. *Life Story of Rasmus B. Anderson, written by himself with the assistance of Albert O. Barton.* Madison, 1917.

Barry, Colman James. *The Catholic Church and German Americans.* (Catholic University of America, *Studies*, Vol. XL.) Washington, D.C., 1953.

Berryman, John R. *History of the Bench and Bar of Wisconsin.* Vol. 1. Chicago, 1898.

The Biographical Dictionary and Portrait Gallery of Representative Men of Chicago, Wisconsin. Chicago and New York, 1895.

Blied, Benjamin J. *Three Archbishops of Milwaukee.* Milwaukee, 1955.

Campbell, Henry C., ed. *Wisconsin in Three Centuries, 1634-1903.* Vols. 4 and 5 (Biographical). New York, 1906.

Desmond, Humphrey J. *The A.P.A. Movement, A Sketch.* Washington, 1912.

Dictionary of Wisconsin Biography. Madison, 1960.

Ellis, John Tracy, ed. *Documents of American Catholic History.* Milwaukee, 1962.

———. *The Life of James Cardinal Gibbons, Archbishop of Baltimore, 1834-1921.* 2 Vols. Milwaukee, 1952.

Evening Wisconsin Newspaper Reference Book. Milwaukee, 1914.

Fowler, Dorothy Ganfield. *John Coit Spooner, Defender of Presidents.* New York, 1961.

Griswold, Ada Tyng, comp. *Annotated Catalogue of Newspaper Files in the Library of the State Historical Society of Wisconsin.* Madison, 1911.

Hattstaedt, Otto F. *History of the Southern Wisconsin District of the Evangelical Lutheran Synod of Missouri, Ohio, and Other States.* St. Louis, 1928. (Trans. Wis. Hist. Records Survey, W.P.A. Madison, 1941.)

Haugen, Nils P. *Pioneer and Political Reminiscences.* Evansville, Wis., 1929. (Reprinted from the *Wis. Mag. of Hist.*, vols. XI, XII, XIII.)

Heming, Harry H. *History of the Catholic Church in Wisconsin.* Milwaukee, 1896.

Herberg, Will. *Protestant–Catholic–Jew.* New York, Doubleday Anchor Paperback, 1960.

Higham, John. *Strangers in the Land.* New Brunswick, N.J., 1955.

Hoffman's Catholic Directory. Milwaukee, 1889.

Ireland, John. *The Church and Modern Society.* Chicago and New York, 1896.

McDonald, Justille. *History of the Irish in Wisconsin in the Nineteenth Century.* Washington, 1954.

Niebuhr, H. Richard. *The Social Sources of Denominationalism.* Cleveland and New York, Meridian Paperback, 1964.

Olson, Oscar Nils. *The Augustana Lutheran Church in America, 1860-1910: The Formative Period.* Davenport, Iowa, 1965,

Patzer, Conrad E. *Public Education in Wisconsin.* Madison, 1924.

Plumb, Ralph G. *Badger Politics, 1836–1930.* Manitowoc, Wis., 1930.

Raney, William F. *Wisconsin, A Story of Progress.* New York, 1940.

Ranking, George W. *William Dempster Hoard.* Fort Atkinson, Wis., 1925.

Report of the Annual Meeting of the Wisconsin Bar Association of 1900. Madison, 1901.

Schlinkert, Leroy, comp. *Subject Bibliography of Wisconsin History.* Madison, 1947.

Smith, Alice E., ed. *Guide to the Manuscripts of the Wisconsin Historical Society.* Madison, 1944.

Soldiers' and Citizens' Album of Biographical Record. Vol. 2. Chicago, 1890.

Stearns, John W. *The Columbian History of Education in Wisconsin.* Milwaukee, 1893.

Stellhorn, August C. *Schools of the Lutheran Church—Missouri Synod.* St. Louis, 1963.

Still, Bayrd. *Milwaukee. The History of a City.* Madison, 1965.

Stokes, Anson Phelps and Pfeffer, Leo. *Church and State in the United States.* New York, Evanston, and London, 1964.

Thomson, Alexander M. *A Political History of Wisconsin.* Milwaukee, 1900.

Usher, Ellis B. *Wisconsin, Its Story and Biography, 1848–1913.* 8 Vols. Chicago and New York, 1914.

Woman's Christian Temperance Union. *Minutes of the Seventeenth Annual Meeting of the Woman's Christian Temperance Union of Wisconsin, Held June 3, 4, 5 and 6, 1890, First Methodist Church, Racine, Wisconsin.* Madison, 1890.

Williams, T. Harry, Current, Richard N., and Freidel, Frank. *A History of the United States [since 1865].* New York, 1960.

Williams Publishing Company. *Notable Men of Wisconsin.* Milwaukee, 1902.

Articles

Azarias, Brother. "Religion in Education," *American Catholic Quarterly Review,* XVI (1891), 760-776.

Barbas, Brother. "Professor Fisher on 'Unsectarianism' in the Common Schools," *Am. Cath. Quart. Rev.*, XIV (1889), 505-515.

Bascom, John. "A New Policy for the Public Schools," *Forum,* XI (March, 1891), 59-66.

Becker, Thomas. "Secular Education," *Am. Cath. Quart. Rev.*, XVII (1892), 176-190.

Bruncken, Ernest. "The Political Activity of Wisconsin Germans, 1854-60," Wis. Hist. Soc. *Proceedings, 1901* (Madison, 1901), pp. 190-211.

Chatard, Francis J. "Are Catholics Right?" *Am. Cath. Quart. Rev.*, XV (1890), 566-575.

"Compulsory English Education: The Bennett Law in Wisconsin," *Public Opinion,* IX (April 12, 1890), 1-4.

Everest, Kate A. "How Wisconsin Came By Its Large German Element," Wis. Hist. Soc. *Collections,* XII (Madison, 1892), 299-334.

Gerberding, G. H. "Reminiscent Pioneering and Moralizing," *Historical and Reminiscent Sketches: English Evangelical Lutheran Synod of the Northwest, 1891-1916* (n.p., 1916), 36-49.

Gregory, John G. "Foreign Immigration to Wisconsin," Wis. Hist. Soc. *Proceedings, 1901* (Madison, 1901), 137-143.

Hennessy, Michael. "Why Education Should Be Free," *Am. Cath. Quart. Rev.*, XVI (1891), 806-817.

Hense-Jensen, W. "Influence of Germans in Wisconsin," Wis. Hist. Soc. *Proceedings, 1901* (Madison, 1901), 144-147.

Higgins, E.A. "The American State and the Private School," *Catholic World*, LIII (July, 1891), 521-527.

Hobbs, William H. "A Pioneer Movement for Americanization," *The Outlook* (April 24, 1918), 4 pp. Reprint in Kellogg Papers, Wis. Hist. Soc.

Jenkins, Thomas Jefferson. "A.P.A. Conspirators," *Catholic World*, LVII (1893), 685-693.

Kellogg, Louise Phelps. "The Bennett Law in Wisconsin," *Wisconsin Magazine of History*, II (September, 1918), 3-25.

Levi, Kate Everest. "Geographical Origins of German Immigration to Wisconsin," Wis. Hist. Soc. *Collections*, XIV (Madison, 1898), 341-393.

Murphy, John. "The Idea of a Parochial School," *Am. Cath. Quart. Rev.*, XVI (1891), 449-461.

Preston, Thomas S. "American Catholicity," *Am. Cath. Quart. Rev.*, XVI (1891), 396-408.

Schafer, Joseph. "Editorial Comment," *Wis. Mag. of Hist.*, X (June, 1927), 455-461. (Remarks on Whyte's discussion of the Bennett Law controversy in the same issue.)

Schley, B. G. "Compulsory Education in Wisconsin: The Bennett Law," *The Nation*, L (March 20, 1890), 240-241.

Vilas, William F. "'The Bennett Law' in Wisconsin," *Forum*, XII (October, 1891), 196-207.

Whyte, William F. "The Bennett Law Campaign in Wisconsin," *Wis. Mag. of Hist.*, X (1927), 364-390.

―――. "The Settlement of the Town of Lebanon, Dodge County," Wis. Hist. Soc. *Proceedings, 1915* (Madison, 1915), 99-110.

Winston, E. M. "The School Controversy in Illinois," *Forum*, XII (October, 1891), 208-214.

TABLE 1

Native Origin and Population of Foreign-Born Residents of Wisconsin in 1890

Origin	Population in Wisconsin
Germanic Nations	**282,900**
Germany	259,819
Austria	4,856
Holland	6,252
Belgium	4,567
Luxembourg	325
Switzerland	7,181
Scandinavian Nations	**99,838**
Norway	65,696
Sweden	20,157
Denmark	13,885
British Dominions	**99,888**
Canada	33,163
England	23,628
Ireland	33,306
Scotland	5,494
Wales	4,297
Slavic Nations	**32,424**
Poland	17,660
Bohemia	11,999
Russia	2,279
Hungary	486
Latin Nations	**3,189**
France	2,009
Italy	1,123

Statistics provided in U.S. Bureau of the Census, *Eleventh Census of the U.S.–1890: Part I, Population* (Washington, D.C., 1895), pp. 606-07 and 686.

TABLE 2

Percentage of German-Born in Wisconsin's Total Population and in the Total Foreign-Born Population of the State, 1850-1890

Census	German-Born	Percentage of Total State Population	Percentage of Foreign-Born State Population
1850	38,064	11.30	32.4
1860	123,879	15.97	44.7
1870	162,314	15.39	45.0
1880	184,328	14.00	45.0
1890	259,819	15.40	50.0

Figures for the years 1850-1880 published in Kate A. Everest, "How Wisconsin Came by Its Large German Element," in Wis. Hist. Soc. *Collections*, XII (Madison, 1892), 300. Figures for 1890 calculated from U.S. Bureau of the Census, *Eleventh Census of the U.S.—1890: Part I, Population* (Washington, D.C., 1895), pp. 606-609.

TABLE 3

Comparative School Census Statistics for Children of Wisconsin Between the Ages of 7 and 14, 1889-1890

	June 30, 1889	June 30, 1890
Number of such children in the state	284,036	294,970
Number of such children who attended public school 12 weeks or more	210,057	225,468
Number of such children who attended private school 12 weeks or more	33,560	38,508
Total number who attended both public and private school 12 weeks or more	243,617	263,976
Number between 7 and 14 who did not attend any school either public or private 12 weeks or more	40,419	30,994
Total increase in the number of children attending both private and public schools in 1890 over the same population in 1889		20,359
Total decrease in the number of children who attended no school in the period 1889 to 1890		9,425

Figures provided in the "Biennial Report of the State Superintendent of the State of Wisconsin for the Two Years Ending June 30, 1890," *Wisconsin Governor's Message and Accompanying Documents, 1891, I* (Madison, 1891), p. 3.

TABLE 4

Ratio of Democratic Vote in 1890 to Democratic Vote in 1888. Same as to Republican Vote.

Counties	% of Democratic Vote in 1890 to Democratic Vote in 1888	% of Republican Vote in 1890 to Republican Vote in 1888
Adams	68	65
Ashland	78	62
Barron	83	64
Bayfield	61	50
Brown	87	73
Buffalo	107	65
Burnett	69	63
Calumet	87	81
Chippewa	87	67
Clark	116	71
Columbia	91	75
Crawford	96	75
Dane	97	82
Dodge	108	70
Door	94	68
Douglas	101	81
Dunn	101	66
Eau Claire	83	58
Florence	66	70
Fond du Lac	101	76
Forest	58	48
Grant	98	82
Green	94	75
Green Lake	119	76

Continued on next page

Table 4, continued from previous page

Iowa	93	84
Jackson	101	65
Jefferson	99	73
Juneau	98	88
Kenosha	99	81
Kewaunee	97	62
La Crosse	103	79
La Fayette	94	88
Langlade	90	85
Lincoln	133	81
Manitowoc	96	71
Marathon	104	66
Marinette	78	64
Marquette	120	66
Milwaukee	138	88
Monroe	100	76
Oconto	99	68
Oneida	92	91
Outagamie	105	74
Ozaukee	115	54
Pepin	94	65
Pierce	75	63
Polk	84	67
Portage	101	67
Price	105	69
Racine	104	83
Richland	82	76
Rock	97	75
St. Croix	80	71

Continued on next page

Table 4, continued from previous page

Sauk	102	72
Sawyer	43	57
Shawano	123	62
Sheboygan	114	76
Taylor	110	61
Trempealeau	88	61
Vernon	91	67
Walworth	94	70
Washburn	85	59
Washington	108	69
Waukesha	93	82
Waupaca	119	76
Waushara	126	78
Winnebago	118	95
Wood	99	76
TOTAL	103	75

Figures from *The Blue Book of the State of Wisconsin, 1891*, p. 255

TABLE 5
Election Pluralities by County and Party in the Wisconsin Gubernatorial Contest for the Years 1886-1894

	1886		1888		1890		1892		1894	
	(Rusk) Rep.	(Woodward) Dem.	(Hoard) Rep.	(Morgan) Dem.	(Hoard) Rep.	(Peck) Dem.	(Spooner) Rep.	(Peck) Dem.	(Upham) Rep.	(Peck) Dem.
Counties that were 15-30% German										
Buffalo	595					254	119		606	
Calumet		841	451	1028		951		952		501
Dodge		1,807		2,934		4,383		4,202		2,684
Fond du Lac		569		438		1,585		1,241	200	
Green Lake	446		282			390		383	246	
Jefferson		778		1,213		1,977		2,008		985
Lincoln	55		64			497		498		79
Manitowoc		367		1,556		2,182		2,063		575
Marathon		685		1,242		2,109		1,919		226
Marquette	202		132			442		330	422	
Milwaukee	3,464		3,184			6,207	15		8,245	
(City)	(2,703)		(2,154)			(5,299)		(902)	(6,355)	
Outagamie		1,225		1,226		2,153		1,894		277
Ozaukee		1,161		1,270		1,915		1,501		1,026
Sauk	758		743			246	67		957	
Shawano	36		149			895		729	91	
Sheboygan		206		703		2,198		1,504	822	
Washington		876		1,309		1,714		978		274
Winnebago	495		276			578		650	2,568	

Continued on next page

Table 5, continued from previous page

	1886		1888		1890		1892		1894	
	(Rusk) Rep.	(Woodward) Dem.	(Hoard) Rep.	(Morgan) Dem.	(Hoard) Rep.	(Peck) Dem.	(Spooner) Rep.	(Peck) Dem.	(Upham) Rep.	(Peck) Dem.
Counties that were 11-14% German										
Columbia	753		854		209		274		1,330	
Dane	737		434			580		149	1,990	
Kewaunee		1,207		1,168		1,447		1,509		885
La Crosse		406	236			718		103	1,146	
Marinette	523		21			237		158	1,111	
Portage	104		253			602		340	14	
Racine	894		630			150	162		1,462	
Waukesha	290		403			75		22	1,077	
Wood		406		90		536		491	1,123	
Counties that were 8-10% German										
Ashland		115	655		32			190	197	
Brown		667		877		1,145		840	137	
Grant	958		857		166		516		1,332	
Kenosha	53		17			286	51	351	324	
Monroe	450		575			76			658	
Price	312		292			19	199		449	
Taylor	217		65			315		197	283	
Waupaca	1,567		1,605		450		1,179		2,154	
Waushara	1,488		1,600		821		1,309		1,922	

Continued on next page

Table 5, continued from previous page

	1886		1888		1890		1892		1894	
	(Rusk) Rep.	(Woodward) Dem.	(Hoard) Rep.	(Morgan) Dem.	(Hoard) Rep.	(Peck) Dem.	(Spooner) Rep.	(Peck) Dem.	(Upham) Rep.	(Peck) Dem.
Counties that were less than 8% German										
Adams	628		670		421		559		797	
Barron	488		913		416		1,003		1,335	
Bayfield		36	497		168		30		738	
Burnett	412		422		264		348		564	
Chippewa		518	175			379		623	542	
Clark	470		977		107		308		1,078	
Crawford	191		244			147	115		497	
Door	781		649		83		554		1,008	
Douglas	1		405		216		601		1,587	
Dunn	1,005		1,224		345		897		1,628	
Eau Claire	229		819			137	290		1,070	
Florence	262		78		63		249		279	
Forest		56	15			14		18	95	
Green	398		503			23	240		656	
Iowa	237		235			13		86	491	
Jackson	917		1,093		364		877		1,261	
Juneau	297		429		208			85	548	
La Fayette	391		279		125		72		489	
Langlade		112		415		416		445		18

Continued on next page

Table 5, continued from previous page

	1886		1888			1890		1892		1894	
	(Rusk) Rep.	(Woodward) Dem.	(Hoard) Rep.	(Morgan) Dem.		(Hoard) Rep.	(Peck) Dem.	(Spooner) Rep.	(Peck) Dem.	(Upham) Rep.	(Peck) Dem.
Counties that were less than 8% German, continued											
Oconto	283		159							429	
Oneida		(no figures)		104			253		253	581	
Pepin	433		465			166	106	425	179	576	
Pierce	1,217		1,325			701		1,075		1,651	
Polk	1,137		1,122			647		851		1,077	
Richland	665		723			449		504		951	
Rock	2,215		2,684			1,218		1,766		3,062	
St. Croix	435		618			254		284		749	
Sawyer		276	34			87		81		15	
Trempeleau	809		709			14		587		1,092	
Vernon	1,543		1,781			812		1,654		2,549	
Walworth	1,924		2,411			1,288		1,763		2,528	
Washburn	87		151				4	150		203	
Total Plurality	18,718		20,273				28,320	7,707		53,900	

Figures compiled from election statistics provided in *The Blue Book of the State of Wisconsin, 1887*, pp. 209-249; *1889*, pp. 202-249; *1891*, pp. 202-257; *1893*, pp. 212-261; *1895*, pp. 212-266.

About the Author

Janet Wegner Johnston is presently a freelance author and editor residing in Casa Grande, Arizona. In that capacity, she has written and edited curriculum guides for students and teachers at several colleges throughout the country.

Janet graduated summa cum laude from the University of Wisconsin at Madison in 1964 with a bachelor's degree in American history and English, earned a master's degree in history from Brown University in 1966, and completed her Ph.D. in political science and public policy at the University of Chicago in 1979 as a U.S. Civil Service Fellow.

Dr. Johnston began her career with the federal government in 1966 as a management intern and was assigned first to the White House Task Force on the Spanish Speaking under President Lyndon B. Johnson and later to the Office of Manpower Policy, Evaluation, and Research in the U.S. Department of Labor in Washington, D.C. After several years working as a program analyst and manpower development specialist in various offices within the Labor Department, she went on to become Chief of the Manpower

Reports Group and Editor-in-Chief of *The Employment and Training Report of the President*, which was transmitted from the White House to the Congress annually.

In 1980, the new Director of the National Commission for Employment Policy (NCEP), which consisted of fifteen presidential appointees representing business, industry, labor, education, state and local governments, and other groups with an interest in guiding federal employment and training policies, invited Janet to become a member of his staff. While at NCEP, she researched and wrote numerous policy papers and authored the first national evaluation of the Job Training Partnership Act (JTPA), based on information gathered from field visits throughout the country and a review of written program evaluations.

Then, after working at the Commission as a senior policy analyst and associate director of research for nearly a decade and authoring many reports and evaluations of federal training programs, Janet was detailed to the Arizona Employment and Training Council (AETC) in Phoenix in 1989 to assist with evaluation and policy development at the state level. Based on her work while at the AETC, Janet received the Governor's Certificate of Merit for Four Years of Outstanding Service to the State of Arizona, the State Job Training Partnership Act Award for Outstanding Work on Behalf of the Citizens of Arizona, and two Governor's Certificates of Appreciation for her work at the Council.

In 1994, having returned to Washington, D.C., she was named Executive Director of the National Commission for Employment Policy. Janet retired from the federal government in 1995 in order to rejoin her husband in Arizona.